PINK
HAIRED
MERMAID
BABY
JESUS

D1516603

Rev. Katy Steinberg

CONTENTS

PREFACE

O ff an insignificant, tree-lined neighborhood street in the small town of Ormond Beach, FL, sits an unsuspecting grouping of warehouses hemmed in on one side by an active set of train tracks. The first time I drove back there, I had visions of movie scenes where people are kidnapped and taken to some vacant, dirty warehouse to be ransomed or other heinous activity. But rounding the bend in the back of the complex, there is often an explosion of activity. Food trucks, live music, a patio full of people, and craft brews slung by a host of local characters wise in the ways of good drink and hospitality. The possibility of all being silenced by a passing train is just part of the charm of this unsuspecting gathering place.

Each year, on the cool evening of December 24th, people young and old bring some of their favorite home-cooked dishes to this local hangout. There's also a bin of varied costumes (shepherds, wisemen, angels and… chickens?) and a handsome, bearded narrator (craft beer in hand), all there to share in community fun and an ancient story of miracles. Children of all ages rush to the raised stage, occupied by local musicians in normal circumstances, to select a costume and take part in the well-known tale of Christmas nativity—sort of.

While organizing for this unique celebration of family, hope, love, joy and new life in unexpected places in 2018, terror struck the hearts of its organizers (Okay, maybe not terror, but like not great either) as we realized we forgot the BABY JESUS! Like any good millennial, we put the call out on social media for someone to bring us a baby Jesus for our local-brewery-pot-luck-unrehearsed-nativity reenactment. Perhaps we shouldn't have been surprised when what showed up, brought by a couple of beloved, self-proclaimed atheists, was a pink-haired mermaid doll. None the less, she was quickly scooped up, swaddled and thrust into the starring role.

That memorable Christmas Eve in 2018 went off with its messy, funny, authentic version of normal, complete with a crunch time pass from one angel to another of our swaddled pink-haired, mermaid baby Jesus. It's far from normal, it's far from accurate, it's far from the high church pageantry many of us experienced in our youth. And somehow, it is sacred in this uncontrived, highly tangible way that makes no logical sense. It engages unexpected (unsuspecting?) people in potent ancient stories, and in a broad and welcoming sense of community. And oh, the laughter! Beautiful, holy laughter.

Welcome to an adventure in embracing holy mess, in divine experimentation, unconventional community and to an incarnational church-ing in all its beautiful and sacred imperfection. Welcome to an exploration of finding God in the unexpected and the holiness of our passions. Welcome to whole cities becoming holy ground as we point to Spirit at work in the everyday. Welcome to Missing Peace.

INTRODUCTION

W hen I think about the main character of the gospels, the man Christians call savior, I can't help but think of the very tangible, physical, earthy, hands-on ministry he led. He was out in the community, preaching and teaching, even when it wasn't well received or popular. He was being edgy and doing new things. He was cavorting with the outsiders and outcasts. This naturally draws me to the contrast of that and my own experiences of church.

I grew up as the daughter of a Presbyterian (PCUSA) pastor. We attended church every Sunday as you might expect, as everyone expected. We sat in large sanctuaries with high arched ceilings made of beautifully polished wood. Hexagonal lantern-style light fixtures hung from above. In my child eyes, there were endless rows of pews cut through with a miles long red-carpeted aisle. Walking down that aisle, the disciples and various gospel stories looked out at me from stained glass windows on either side. An elevated stage, they called it a chancel (cause church), accessed by two small, red carpeted steps resided at the front of the sanctuary thronged by a pulpit and lectern, and hemmed in from the rear by the choir loft. Above the choir, a large rose window depicting various biblical characters and their stories filled the majority of the wall. And last but not least, a golden cross, several feet in length, rose high above it all.

Church folks insisted that church was not a building, but a people. But child me knew better. When we gathered outside of that building, they didn't call it *church*. They could tell me all they wanted, but I knew what church was. Why else would they have made so much effort to create this specially adorned space unless *it* was literally the church?

I also remember being told it was God's house. So, not only did I know that church was a building, it was where God lived. It was where you found God, once a week, for an hour and no more so we could, "beat the Baptists to lunch."

My dad was a good pastor of that church. His sermons were eloquent and thoughtful, spoken in a booming voice seemingly made for just that purpose. He loved his congregation and spent endless hours listening to their stories, meeting them for lunch or visiting them in the hospital. And by and large, they treated me like family.

I don't think I ever heard a directly exclusive message in church. I think Presbyterians are pretty good at not saying the wrong things, but I'm not sure we are as good at saying the right things, especially if they might offend some. We made the gospel really nice, and it lived in this nice house we built for it—God's house. This naturally meant that people who were not here weren't part of that. There were subtle hints of rivalry between denominations. And then there were the requirements to be a member, and another layer of them to partake in sacraments (communion and baptism).

On one hand, I get it. There has to be some requirements so that we aren't diluting the meaning of these holy things. And. Now. I don't believe that reflects the abundant and unconditional love of God. And if we aren't to find that in the church—God's house—then where are we to find it?

Perhaps this is the question that has driven so many from the church (along with a host of others, I'm sure). Certainly, the alienating factor I've heard most revolves around hypocrisy. To say these churches are God's house, then have these people hold the keys and decide who is in and out, and these people decide who is welcome at the table and who is not, and by the way it differs in each of God's houses—it all gets a bit off-putting. Or maybe a lot off-putting. And maybe you're willing to let it slide a bit, until one of the people left out is you, or someone you love. Then it starts to feel less and less like it has anything to do with God at all.

This is not the particular point in history when God decided to show up somewhere besides church buildings. My friend Zac Morton says nature is God's original gospel, God's original love letter. The first story in the Bible would seem to agree. Creating and then proclaiming creation's goodness, over and over and over. We had always been taught some version of "God is everywhere." Sometimes with a warning about our behavior…we were being watched…but also nudging us toward an idea that we might meet God elsewhere. Ya know, besides God's house. Or, what was increasingly feeling to me, God's beautiful, steeple-laden, stained glass casket.

So, we've got this earthy, walk-among-the-people, healing, story-telling, homeless, heavily criticized son of man and these giant, beautiful, wealthy, well kempt, stationary, exclusive churches. The dissonance is strong. And the space between these two seems very fertile ground for something new.

Let me be clear, I love the church of my childhood, and it loved me well. And at the same time, I can see so clearly the space for something more incarnational, more fleshy. Something that looks outward more, or at least as much, as inward. Something so authentic, dynamic, healing story-telling, and even heavily criticized, that it matches the story of Jesus so much more readily than the church of my childhood did or does.

On a Sunday afternoon in 2015, a small group of people decided to take a shot at it. It was a warm autumn day in August, and 16 unchurched and/or dechurched people, curious about a different way to come together around and engage with God/Universe/Spirit, gathered in my humble kitchen in walls adorned with giant post-its. We shared ideas, asked questions and experimented with a new way to think about faith.

We wanted to use our strength, nurture our spirit and serve our community. As the smells of breakfast lingered in the air, and dirty dishes in the sink, we wondered about a relationship with God outside of the religious structures we'd been alienated from. We wondered about a spiritual community that would be different, a highly incarnational, highly inclusive version of church-ish. Like "a church for people who don't go to church," as one of our youngest participants offered. One that was more about relationship than religion.

We would call this spiritual experiment Missing Peace. Honoring that we all need more peace, whatever we believe. Acknowledging that each of us, in some way, is missing peace and that each of us, in some way, is a missing piece. We would get a fuller picture of the holy by experiencing how each of us recognizes Spirit. Each of us could bring a piece (a peace), and we would learn to see God in so much more. By sharing the most meaningful ways we get a taste of the divine, we all grow.

As it turns out, there is a scripture, a teaching, a hope that Jesus seemed to hold above all others. "You shall love the Lord your God with all your heart, and with all your soul, and with all your strength, and with all your mind; and your neighbor as yourself" (Luke 10:27)—a version of which is found in 27 different places in scripture, making it one of the most prominently featured teachings in all of the Bible. What if that was our model for participating in relationship with the divine in community? Missing Peace decided it would try.

We dared to try and capture these three ways to love, or be in relationship, with God as "spiritual" (heart and soul), "physical" (strength), "cerebral" (mind) and "service" (the loving of neighbor). Each time we gathered, we would emphasize one of these pillars with some framing thoughts and an activity to highlight them. Though we don't truly believe them separate, by emphasizing one, we can see all four more clearly and the ways they overlap and integrate in our shared humanity. We'd have to be nomadic, gathering in parks, beaches, museums, city buildings, coffee shops, homeless shelters, campgrounds, restaurants; as many places where people are experiencing the divine as possible. We'd have to do different activities like surfing, painting, picking up trash, discussions, kickball, labyrinth walks, poetry, art; as many activities wherein people are experiencing the divine as possible, and hear the stories of as many people's authentic experiences of the divine as possible.

My intention with this book is to invite you into how Missing Peace is discovering more and new faith through expanding our definition of worship in our spiritual laboratory. I'll share stories of the four areas (spiritual, physical, cerebral and service) that Jesus and Missing Peace emphasize for being in relationship with the divine and what we are discovering about worshipping in each of these ways. My deep hope is that it will inspire those who have become disenchanted with church as they know it…whether they wear a robe and stole each week or haven't ventured into a church service in years. Among these stories, I hope God will speak to you and invite you into new and exciting ways of relationship. May your heart be opened, your mind engaged, your spirit alive and love be the outcome. Amen.

For more on Missing Peace, check out missingpeacecommunity.com or search for us on YouTube, Facebook, Instagram and/or Twitter.

Part 1:

LET'S GET PHYSICAL – LOVING WITH OUR STRENGTH

But first, a story...

My husband Jeff is one of the many who have fallen in love with CrossFit. He stumbled upon a local gym, or "box" as I'm told they're called, and was hooked. My "not a morning person" husband began getting up at 5:00am to go work out, something he'd not done in our previous 10+ years together. Despite being someone who has always valued fitness, he'd never been so committed. What was it about this particular type of fitness that so captured him?

I finally asked him. He, of course, mentioned the endorphins and feeling good after a good work out, but there was something else. There's something about the culture of CrossFit, a culture that fosters a sense of community and encouragement. One where people journey together toward the very edge of their capacity. A culture that finds strength in each other when the individual seems to have nothing left. I was beginning to smell something spiritual happening.

Jeff introduced me to the owner of the box of which he is a member, and I began to ask her a multitude of questions about CrossFit. What makes it different from other fitness regimens? How do they foster a sense of community? Why are those things important? And, perhaps my most driving question, is there a sense of something else happening in that space? Does it feel spiritual? To which she emphatically answered, yes!

From that point, the East Ormond Beach CrossFit owner, Melissa Kiel, and I began to dream about what it might look like to partner. Melissa is an expert at this very physical thing with a nod to the spiritual or "something else" that happens at CrossFit, and I was focused on this very spiritual thing with a nod to the physical at Missing Peace. Maybe we could together build something that created space for a deep expression of both.

With the permission of another community with the same name, we formed "With All Our Strengths." We'd meet on Sunday for a customized workout that would point to a topic, like perseverance, and I would prepare a scripture-based meditation around the same topic. Together, we would curate space for a mindful, intentional, physical experience of the divine in community. Or, as I like to call it: church.

CHAPTER 1

What does it mean for us to worship God with our strength as Luke 10:27, etc. seems to beckon us to do? I'd argue it is one of the most neglected ideas by the traditional mainline church; that we would engage our physicality as a means of relationship with God. Perhaps that's because God seems so intangible, and yet, if the central story is about word made flesh (incarnation), the physical existence is a major and important component of who we are in our divine heritage.

What is worship through our physical self? I've wondered aloud on more than one occasion what it would look like for a muscle to worship. The best I can fathom is, by doing what it was created to do. It would push and pull. It would move things. It would work hard and grow. It would be exactly what a muscle should be. We wouldn't expect it to do things it couldn't. We wouldn't ask it to talk like a mouth or breathe like lungs in order to be faithful to its calling.

With the muscle idea as our guide, how would we, a whole person, worship with our physicality? We would do what our physicality was made to do. Run, play, exercise, move in challenging ways and in joyful ways, together. But if it were to be something more, something deeper than just playing together (a valuable thing in and of itself), there would need to be some intentionality. There would need to be some liturgy to set the tone. There would need to be some framing of what it had to do with life, faith and community. If we wanted these physical activities to create space for spiritual evolution, they would have to be more than just a thrown together game. There must be an invitation to pay deep attention in and through these activities for the "something deeper" going on.

Jesus often looked to his environment and culture for how people might understand these deeper, spiritual, intentional, living-into-calling, God things. So, how might we look to the collaborative, playful, really human ways we live out our physicality to teach us something about God, the kingdom and the meaning and hope of life? We would honor the fact that some kind of magic happened naturally when people played together or exercised together, and we would emphasize that by inviting people to pay really deep and present attention in the midst of it.

The CrossFit phenomenon and upwelling of kickball leagues are obvious examples of people longing to engage their physicality in community. Yes, for the fun of it, but also for this unnamable, intangible thing that keeps drawing people back. These activities are intentionally about physicality, but they sort of nod to "something else." They hint at "something deeper" that happens when people gather together and experience joy and challenge.

As our culture seems to be losing its sense of community, or at least moving it to online forums that lack the same interactive connectivity of an in-person relationship, we find ourselves deeply hungry for in-real-life human experiences together. A hunger rooted in our divine heritage that calls us into community with each other and God. A hunger independent of whether we openly acknowledge God or just the something meaningful we sense when we gather. We desire to journey together, and physical activity together is a version of that in miniature, in a way we can complete in about an hour together. Missing Peace is venturing its guess, experimenting with the possibility of this journey together through physical activity as worshiping God with our strength.

Unlike the worship experiences of my youth, laugh-out-loud joy is an appropriate part of relationship with our heavenly parentage (i.e.

worship)! Let's experiment with joyful, physical, expressions of that relationship—bridging the gap between God and humanity in our deep, gasping breaths, physical exertions and inevitable laughter. We don't have to make it up. Like Jesus so frequently referenced the world, culture and activities of his time, we can lean on the experiences of everyday people engaged in joyful and challenging practices that keep drawing them back into meaningful community. Practices that have a hold on them far more than a standard trip to the gym. Practices that create space for sensing the Spirit when busyness is set aside.

What is it about these activities that engage and draw people, that give them a sense of who they are? What was going on that made this so meaningful and engaging? How did they feel in the midst of it? What were they experiencing in their heart of hearts? Why did these activities matter? There's really only one way to find out: ask! The very people who are having these divine experiences through their physical activities are the ones who can teach us about why. They can teach us about how God is present, or how their experience of awe and wonder are provoked, or when they feel alive through physical activity. People are already getting a sniff, a little sip, in their everyday explorations of these activities, but what if we could intentionally emphasize that "something else," that God component, as a way of worshiping with our strength.

In order to curate space where physical activity becomes worship, we would listen to the stories of people. Ask where they felt close to God. Ask what it was like and why. Ask if they'd be willing to share it with the community to show, teach, share with us the activities that generated that sense of the holy.

One of our Missing Peacers had the idea to do archery together as one of our physical expressions of worship. Initially, I sensed some very apparent metaphors about when we hit and miss the target, and how each effort, whether it lands or not, is making you better. But that's not the fullness of where it went. When I met with the originator of the idea, he had a whole other take on the value of the archery experience, what it meant to him, how it connected him with God and how he found this experience meaningful enough that he wanted to share how it affected him and invite others into it. This is how we wanted to be Missing Peace, by engaging how each one experiences the Divine and emphasize it by doing it in intentional community.

What I learned about the experience of archery connected so beautifully with the gospel I knew and loved. It was my deep hope that with a bit of framing, the magical experience of finding God in the physical act of archery, could be highlighted with the teachings of scripture and vice versa, thus revealing God in a new way. Breathing new life into the beauty of our humanity and all the ways God can find us in the midst of these unexpected spaces, or at least create space for that possibility. With Jesus as our example, it just made sense to look to the physical world, the places people were already finding God, for new ways to live into the Divine/human relationship.

So, we gathered on a frosty (for Florida anyway) January morning. A group of about 15 people circled up on the property of our host. He'd set up a small campfire to help us stay warm, and the nostalgic smell of burning wood welcomed us into community, evoking a sense of youthful summer camp connection. A couple of different targets and types of bows and arrows were set up so the experience could be inclusive for even the smallest amongst us. The grass was damp, our breath was visible, the air was still, anticipation was ripe.

After the initial (and inevitable for a nomadic community) gathering time, we walked through our practices of prayer and breath and community statement (more on this later) as we gathered around our fragrant campfire. I gave a framing sermon (below), which felt to me like an echo of ancient sharings around campfires as far back as humanity goes. Then we did archery together and embodied the ideas we had just talked about. We engaged the gifts of the people, their real-life gifts and how they experience God, together as a community. We had varying "success" at the sport, but unvarying connection with each other. And the gospel sunk into my bones in a new way. It felt like a restored, renewed version of church. Like what it could be – joy, laughter, humanity, the divine, holy space, connection, all of it.

Sermon from our archery experience:

Archery

(https://youtu.be/g3FOVodYYaU)

"The earliest found proof of archery dates back to 9 to 10 thousand BC. That's almost unfathomable. People were shooting arrows 6 to 7 thousand years before they were writing language. People were stringing bows almost 11 thousand years before they were speaking English.

When most people think of this ancient art form, they think of it for war or for hunting. But that is not all that it is or can be. The Japanese practice of Kyudo (kai-oo-doe), which means 'the way of the bow,' is seen as a craft 'synonymous with the pursuit of truth, goodness and beauty.'[i] Kyudo compares archery to yoga, claiming the unification of the mental and physical in its practice, but has the added benefit of teaching focus, discipline and precision with immediate feedback provided by the target.

Look, I've heard over and over in my life as a follower and believer people saying 'I don't need to go to church, I find God...' fill in the blank, on the golf course, on the water, at the beach, in nature, etc. And I think that is really possible...that claim coincides well with what we are doing at Missing Peace as we look for God in all aspects of who we are. However, while I think God can be found there, I'm not sure we always look. It's like we say about our breathing together...most of our life is done in these shallow sips of air that just get us by. But, boy, are we missing out if we never breathe deeply.

That is why we gather. Not because you can't find God elsewhere; you can...I pray that you do and you will, but it is a different experience. It is shallow sips of God that just get us by. The book of Hebrews says it like this, 'And let us consider how we may spur one another on toward love and good deeds, not giving up meeting together, as some are in the habit of doing, but encouraging one another.[ii]*' When we set aside focused time to look and listen for God, when we are intentional, at least for a few moments together, we build off of each other's experiences. We think more deeply. We engage dormant parts of ourselves. We drink deeply, breathe deeply, of the God experience here on earth.*

Jesus was always using people's everyday experiences to teach about who God is and who we are supposed to be, and not, I believe, purely as metaphor—though that is a helpful and powerful tool—but also because God is present in these things. God is making them new, renewing and resurrecting the trees between winter and spring, inspiring awe through the mountain ranges, imbuing food and drink with the power to draw people together, and so much more.

Our event today is the brainchild of Clint, who is our host along with Megan. When we talked more about archery, what he loves about it, why he wanted to share it, I once again saw these beautiful tendrils of God-stuff creeping in. See, when an archer is on the hunt, there is a certain oneness that happens with the environment and with the target. Senses are heightened, you can see, hear and smell more clearly as you focus in—a deep, world-ignoring focus. Every breath is slow, deep, measured. The shot requires an almost intimate proximity to the animal and a stealthiness that levels the playing field between hunter and hunted. The disciplined hunter will wait for the right shot, honoring the wind, terrain, creature, all with barely a conscious thought. Then the time comes to release the arrow. The hunter sees the arrow hit the target in the mind's eye long before it meets its fate in the real world, and more often than not, the result is a miss. A miss? Why go on this journey if more often than not, it's a miss? Because it's not about perfection. It's not about hitting every target, it's instead about the experience, the intensity, the subtle lessons taught to the mind and the body, the hope of using those lessons toward a better outcome next time, and the connection with both the fellow hunter and prey for the journey they've been on together. See, for a committed archer, archery will be a lifelong pursuit that never promises a steady return of prey, but always promises to shape the archer.

And so it is with the journey we are on together. No one here will promise you a steady return of external reward from our time together, but like the archer, you are shaped each time by your experience and the oneness with each other and our target—God. So, do I believe you can find God out on your boat, on the golf course, in your children's eyes? Hell yeah I do. But the journey we take together, the ways we engage in an intentional recognition of God at work in the world, the thing that brings us back again and again, is what will sharpen your and my ability to see God elsewhere too...heightening your sense and awareness each time we hunt. How incredibly grateful I am to journey with you all."

By Clint lending his eyes, his view of finding God in the everyday, the rest of us were welcomed into it in a new way. For some folks, this hit home in a way no Sunday school lesson ever could. For others, it was a bit of a miss. For all we learned about each other and about a new way to experience God, and hopefully, a new lens through which to find God in our own every day.

And we lived into it. We weren't just inspired with an idea that would eventually get washed away with the normal business of life. We took the idea and made it flesh, right there together, thus freeing us from the ideal and placing us firmly in the actual. An echo of word made flesh. A nod to our imperfect existence and every idea that both loses and gains immeasurably in the enacting of it. A holy living into the divine image of creator.

There's a reason that the things that bring people joy, bring them joy.

It's not purely the activity itself; it's the way the Spirit is present in it. It's the way that God knows God's children and how to invite them into a loving embrace. It's the way the universal Christ shows us love through that joy. And shouldn't it be the role of the "church" to point to that, to highlight it, to encourage people in that joy and create the space to live it out? At Missing Peace, we think yes.

CHAPTER 2

Another idea that arose for Missing Peace and our physical expression of worship was kickball. I don't remember where it came from, perhaps one of the kids…perhaps a kid at heart. But the idea of finding God and connecting with each other through play was obvious for us. The way that the holy is so tangible in the act of play, and not in a solemn, quiet way, but in a loud, boisterous, laughing kind of way just struck a chord. At some point on the journey to adulthood, we part with that childlike sense of trust, giddiness, playful abandon that is particularly potent in play. A rare space not dedicated to productivity or a purpose. This is a space where divinity and humanity boldly intersect. There is so much humanity can learn from how children play, with little preference of who the playmates are, fearlessly, much like I imagine heaven—a heaven both already and not yet. And so, we play together.

When it comes to kickball specifically, it begs the question: what on earth could kickball have to do with the gospel, with the teachings of a rabbi who lived millennia before kickball was invented? With the human experience and hope and love and Spirit? I see it as a divine gifting that this community sees with supernatural vision how God is present in even the most surprising activities. Breath, sweat, laughter, effort—each of these is a part, though often neglected, of the fullness of the human experience. Missing Peace is convinced God/love/Universe wants the fullness of the human experience for us. All of this is present in play, in a game of kickball if we are but open to it.

It's not a big leap to connect this idea with the ancient story of word made flesh—of idea, logos, love becoming one with humanity in all its humanness (John 1:14), and Jesus' repeated invitations into the fullness of that through meals, growing things and playing together. In short, it's about embracing what it means to be human, just as he did. So, why not kickball? Why not a joyful game played in community? Might this too shape who we are in our divine image?

There's a park in Ormond Beach, kind of right in the middle of town, but just off the busy roads. It's aptly named Central Park and encompasses about 150 acres including two lakes. There are trails, pavilions, a fitness path, a labyrinth, playgrounds, tennis courts, a community garden and plenty of wide-open spaces for play. Nestled at the northern end of the park, off of a treelined, quiet road, is a little field with one of these playgrounds, a pavilion and parking lot.

Often on a Sunday morning, a rag tag group of 15 or so (about half under the age of 10) will gather in this common and sacred space. Right in among the cobwebs and dog mess. The fresh air and damp grass. The bird calls and frog ribbits. The holy and the earthly. We throw a couple of bright-orange rubber bases in a rough diamond formation on the field—more concerned with little legs making it than regulation size—and we circle up to connect, both with each other and the holy intention of the day.

The group divides up into loose teams, and there's a potent mixture of the competitiveness of adults approaching middle age (and beyond) and the innocence of the children and our desire for them to have fun. Score is very loosely kept, both teams win—well, if you ask the kids, the adults have secretly kept score the whole time. Slips, misses, laughter, squeals, gentleness, effort; all of it happens. And it is good (Genesis 1:31).

Sermon from kickball experience

Kickball and the Kingdom

(https://youtu.be/CXvF-CvFQIo)

"In preparation for this week, I couldn't help but think about joy—childlike joy. The simple, pure pleasure of life without the invasive worry and fear we cultivate over our lifetimes.

I'm reminded of a great story from the book of Matthew. The entourage, I mean disciples, are arguing. And I try to give them a break here because the stuff Jesus is talking about is so foreign. Everything they know is based in a caste system where the family you are born into and the order in which you were born decide your whole life. There is no such thing as upward mobility, and don't even get me started on what it was like for women.

All that to say, they had a lot of questions when Jesus started talking about a different world order, a different kingdom, where class and family name and birth order didn't matter. Where what did matter was being kind to one another and promoting peace and sharing what you have. How would decisions be made? Who would be in charge?

The funny thing is, Jesus didn't make up these ideas; he pulled them right out of the ancient sacred texts of these Middle Eastern people. It just didn't seem real or true in light of their circumstances, in light of a system where they said one thing and did another, where they talked about being good and holy and taking care of the foreigner among them but didn't do it. Wow. This sometimes makes me feel like we've made no progress at all.

Back to the entourage, they're trying to figure out who will be given highest rank in this new world, in this new kingdom Jesus is describing. See, they're applying their earthly thinking to heavenly concepts. And it's foolishness. It's like trying to apply the laws of physics to matters of love. It just doesn't work. So, Jesus, in his classic world-changing,

Jesus-y way, calls to a child and brings the kid over in front of everyone. And he says, unless you become like this child, unless you become humble and joyful and peaceful and trusting and loving and stop worrying about things that just don't matter, unless you become like this child, you'll never enter the kingdom.

Now, I really don't believe this to be a threat of heaven and hell as I've heard it interpreted. What I hear in this is a call to us all to engage in this life with child-like joy. To not allow the realities of this world or the social order of this world or who this world tells us we ought to be to look and feel successful. But instead, to live into the kingdom that Jesus describes, where the first is the last, and everyone is cared for, and there are no orphans or lonely widows but real community where we all give of ourselves when we have it to give and lean on the collective when we don't. That's the kingdom.

But sometimes we forget, or its too hard, or the siren song of this world is just too strong to resist, and we buy in to social status and ignore the needs of others and abandon our child-like selves, traded in for the unworthy replacement of worldly values. Thank God for grace, and each other, to help us through that.

So today, as a reminder of what it is like to be a child, as a reminder of joy, as a reminder of humility, as a reminder of trust, as a reminder of hope in the kingdom that Jesus describes, we will play kickball. And we will remember how loved we are and that there is nothing we have to do to earn it, just like these children among us. And we will remember that we live for purposes beyond the ones dictated by this world but instead into the purposes of a God who wants so very much more for God's beloved children."

I've heard it said that the universal is always present in the particular. That, when you are zeroing in on where you find joy, or what really matters, or who you deeply are, there are always connection points. There are universal truths found in the particularities of our existence.

God, Spirit, Christ, love, hope, joy—it's all present in all things, and yet, it can escape us so easily with the cursory glances our busy lives most naturally make space for. So, we must slow down, pay attention, listen and look for where God stands with an open embrace just waiting for us. Never coercing and always inviting us further up and further in to love.

This is what it looks like, this is what it feels like, to love God with our strength. With our full fleshy existence, in our identity as children of God. We move, we breath, we laugh, and we do it together, sensing the Spirit in a way our hearts and minds aren't capable of. In a way that is unique to our physicality. A way that scripture invites us into over and over again (Mark 12:30, 33; Luke 10:27).

Questions for Loving with Your Strength:

1. What physical activities bring you joy?

2. How do you experience God in unexpected places and activities?

3. What might it be like to do the things you love with a holy intentionality?

4. Just as you hope for playful and joyful experiences for the one you love, can you embrace that God wants that for you?

5. What ideas do you have to worship/love God through your strength (physicality)?

Part 2:

WHERE'S THE WOO? – LOVING WITH OUR HEART AND SOUL

But first, a story...

About three and a half years into the life of Missing Peace, we decided to do a series on who we are, what our gifts are and who we will be going forward. As part of this exploration, we used Clifton Strength Finders, Core Values Assessments and other tools to rediscover our identity and mission. Part of the goal of these exercises was also to indicate who we would be going forward. What are our hopes and dreams for this community? What does leadership look like? Where do we go from here?

I felt like I needed a strong ending to the series but had no idea what that would be. On my early morning beach walk, I felt God's gentle nudge in my heart, and it felt like an answer. As my feet fell in the sand and the sun began to warm the Earth below, the rhythms of day and night, summer and winter, life and death were just so...apparent. At Missing Peace, we were shifting too. And all at once, I knew what we needed. A funeral. We needed to eulogize and even mourn all that had gone before if we were going to fully embrace what was to come. We needed a death if there was to be any hope of a resurrection.

As I received this message (for lack of a better descriptor for the experience), I had a lot of questions. What does that mean, God? Is this the end of Missing Peace? In our human world, the only thing that follows a funeral is a long time of embracing and recovering from grief and loss. Or is it? We also learn a new normal. We redefine ourselves in the face of loss.

I don't remember getting answers to my questions about this funeral for Missing Peace, but I did feel sure of the next step. A way to honor an ending. A way to grieve and be made anew. A profound example of gospel teaching/living in echoing the life and death of Jesus— something essential to the foundation of Missing Peace. And so, I planned a funeral.

In my very humanness, I also planned a resurrection (pause for laughter). I thought I could, in a one-hour gathering, have a funeral and then shift gears and plot the way forward. As you may have guessed, this is not what happened.

It was a cool Sunday morning when we gathered at one of our favorite spots on the bank of the Halifax River, surrounded by beautifully manicured gardens and bordered from the road by a large, circular fountain. In this picturesque setting sits an old church building that the city bought and restored for use as a gathering space. While it had been remodeled—pews removed, religion erased—the spirit of the place and its original identity are palpable, and the history of its saints is captured in a series of newspaper clippings framed on the wall.

We collected in a circle of chairs in the small once-sanctuary, sheltered in the embrace of familiar, warm, wood-planked walls and ceiling, and we told stories of Missing Peace. We talked of places we'd gone, things we had learned, what had moved us. Stories that somehow made a new home in wet streaks down our faces. We heralded the transformational moments of our time together. We laughed at the blunders, and we shared just how much Missing Peace had meant to each of us. We affirmed that if this was the end of our story together, it had been a good and meaningful story.

As we approached the end of our time together, there just was no space to think about what was next. We needed to sit in this grief a bit, to "stay dead" a while. So, we did. We didn't plan the next meeting. We didn't make any goals. We left it dead. And we walked out of this once-church and through its beautiful gardens on the bank of the Halifax like people leaving a funeral—still grieving but somehow comforted.

About a week later, I sent out invitations to the community to come to my house for "Resurrection Tacos." An opportunity to come together, over a meal, and feel/wait/look/listen for God's call for us to rise. Or not. A small group gathered, and while we ate, we came to the conclusion that this work is not yet finished. That we will not stay dead. That Missing Peace should live again. And so, we did.

CHAPTER 3

I've found a newly-common phrase of our highly secularized, fast-paced world: *woo*. It's when there's no measurable, tangible, calculated, clearly-accomplishing-the-next-step-and-furthering-your-life way to explain things. It's talk of spiritual things or the practice of them. It's anything that doesn't feel clearly and firmly grounded in this world and its outcome-based culture. Belief. Faith. Hope. Connection. In a word, its spiritual.

Woo could be seen as dismissive, as in, "What made you go all woo?" But it could also be seen as an effort to engage new language around spiritual experience as its primary source in American culture (church) is in decline. It may also be a nod to the nature of spiritual things; that once you try to describe them, they eek out between your fingers like so much sand. It's a hard thing to capture in words, so *woo* is as good as any.

Perhaps the need for a new word comes from the abusive, coercive and/or manipulative "spiritual" experiences so many have experienced. They have been continually encouraged that they just need to pray harder, or believe more, or conform in some way in order to be connected to God. But the hypocrisy in that is strong when compared to the stories of a radical rabbi who was always pointing out God in parable, in the land itself, in children, in things that contradicted the cultural norms. It's not a big wonder why people have been and continue to opt out of this kind of institution. I tend to think Jesus would have too.

If some folks weren't finding God/Universe/Spirit in these places, then where was she? Sure, they/we were getting hints of her in nature, in relationship, in love, in justice, but where and how could we engage more deeply. Where could we experiment with different ways to engage? And what are the ways that each of us was experiencing woo? Where could we find increased emphasis for the spiritual if it weren't in churches where some have felt alienated, excluded, manipulated or otherwise abused?

Missing Peace never intended to capture God and then present what we found. To somehow create an experience of God, or worse, perform one for consumption. We just felt like there needed to be a new kind of space. One intended to be a journey together. Leaning on our own experiences of woo/Spirit/God and those of other people over time captured in scripture, history and story, honoring that we are not the first to seek the deep meaning, the good news, the hope and connection with our divine parentage.

We don't create or produce these experiences, instead we create the space for them. We've sometimes called it curating—like a museum that doesn't create the art but makes space for it. We could craft opportunities and invitations, and trust that God/Universe/Spirit would, once people were paying attention, show up...or was there all along, but we just needed to get still or quiet or otherwise tuned in. Our spiritual practices focus us on just that, on paying attention, getting still (literally or figuratively), opening ourselves to divine possibility and connection. We lean on a myriad of spiritual practices people have engaged over human history. We lean on the scriptures, teachings and ancient practices. We lean on other religions and contemplations and meditations that invite humanity into the thin space, the already and not yet, the kingdom, the woo.

Holding this kind of space is rare in our lives. It seems unproductive (by worldly standards) and indulgent. What are the metrics for success on this thing? How do we know it's working? It's slippery and immeasurable, and yet may just be the most meaningful and formative engagement we can be a part of. It's about holding space for, paying attention to and nurturing our divine essence.

The labyrinth has a long history of creating that woo kind of space. A winding path laid out on the ground. One merely walks, simply following the path. There are no dead ends or tricks, just a simple winding journey in and back out. But it is also a deep metaphor as one wanders its folds. A miniature representation of the larger journey of life. An opportunity to quiet oneself and walk with intention. To pilgrimage into the wonderings and wanderings of your deepest self, to listen for the voice of Spirit, to venture into another realm that does not honor the productivity and efficiency of our culture.

At the section of Central Park where we play kickball, tucked away at the very western end, there is a circular stone pad laid into the ground, maybe 30 feet across. It is connected to the park's sidewalk with a small concrete offshoot and is prettily surrounded by small trees and shrubs that often drop flowers, leaves and berries onto the stone. The circle is inlaid with a winding path that slowly weaves toward and away, toward and away from the center in a series of interlocking folds. They eventually meander to the very heart of the circle where a small stone bench, just wide enough for two, is placed. Back at the entrance to the circle, a small sign shares that this is a labyrinth and beckons the walker to enter with their questions and worries, pause in the middle for silence, and listen on the way out.

As a community, Missing Peace gathers in this place, centers ourselves and prepare our hearts for the journey. We breathe deeply the crisp morning air and listen for the natural sounds of the park—bird, breeze, breath. And then we make our journey in twos and threes into the folds of the labyrinth. We greet each other warmly as we would on the larger journey this one represents. We make space for one another on this personal and communal journey (aren't they all?). And we are unproductive human beings, instead of the normal workaday human doings, making space to pay attention to Spirit. Despite each being in the same space, opportunity and path, each has their own unique journey. And when it is done, we share the stories and discoveries revealed therein.

Sermon from labyrinth experience:

Into the Labyrinth

(https://youtu.be/ItmB489xH0A)

"In preparation for this week, I stumbled into the perfect metaphor for the spiritual practice of walking the labyrinth. Some of you know that we have walked this labyrinth before, both as we examined ways to pray and as a spiritual practice worth examining all on its own. But as I looked for my notes from the last time we used the labyrinth as our spiritual practice, I couldn't find them. You may remember that my house was robbed earlier this year, and one of the things that will never return are the notes and documents from my original laptop. They're just gone, and we have to move on, creating new notes and documents, a new life. Why is this the perfect metaphor? Well, that's what the labyrinth is all about. It's all about moving forward. It's all about letting go of the old and welcoming the new. It's all about realizing how far you've come.

The journey you are about to embark upon into this labyrinth will be a short one, a few minutes at most, but it represents a much larger journey—the journey we take as we live out the entirety of our lives, and the spiritual journeys we take over and over again. As you wander through its folds, part of it will seem familiar, you might find yourself thinking, didn't I just walk here? Did I get turned around? Should I go back the way I came? Just as what happens in our lives as we learn the deepest lessons. Haven't I done this before? How have I not learned this lesson? Is it possible to just turn around, go back the way I came? But, of course, it's not. That won't get you any farther on your journey.

There's this part of us, particularly the older we get, I think, where we long for what is behind us. We romanticize the past and think to ourselves, back when things were…fill in the blank—'easy', 'made sense', 'good', 'healthy.' Man, if I could just go back there. But what we know is we can't. Not and continue to progress and grow and learn. Not and continue to transform. Not and become who we are supposed to be.

See, there are these seasons in our lives, just like in the natural world. And even as we are longing for one season to stop and another to start, or longing for the season just passed, we know that each of them is necessary. Even the particularly long and hot ones. And so it is with life.

The ancient Hebrew poetry that depicts the creation of the world breaks it down into seven parts it refers to as days. Buried in the center of this description, 'day 4' to be exact, is a revealing line about the passage of time, change, the seasons. It says, 'God spoke: "Lights! Come out. Shine in Heaven's sky! Separate Day from Night. Mark seasons and days and years. Lights in Heaven's sky to give light to Earth." And there it was.' See, ancient Hebrew poetry was often written in a chiastic form where they intentionally buried the meaning of the whole thing in the middle. So, anyone reading it in the ancient world would have had that line, centered directly between God beginning creation and God resting, that line about seasons would jump out at them. It's a reminder of the rhythms of nature and the rhythms of life, a reminder that there is a time for producing and a time for rest. A reminder not to long for what has passed but appreciate if for how it creates space for what is to come. A reminder not to get ahead of yourself, because the next season is on its way. A reminder that when its going hard, a season of rest is coming and that when your season feels a little unproductive, another is coming behind that one too[iii].

As you journey through the labyrinth, you'll find places where it doubles back on itself, and it feels like you are going backwards, but you are still on your way to the destination. You'll find long stretches where it feels as if you're just going to go in a circle, but you aren't, you're still moving toward your destination. You'll have moments when you think you are almost there, and the winding turns of the labyrinth will draw you back away. And yet, you are still ever closer to your destination.

The quickest, most efficient way to travel between two points is a straight line. We are surrounded by a straight-line world. But today, I invite you into the folds. The twists and turns. The seemingly going backwards and thinking you're close and being drawn away again...because that is where growth happens. That is where the transformation and revelation happens. That is why we walk the labyrinth of life through all its seasons of plenty and want, of work and stillness, of joy and of pain, of hope and despair. Those are the places that life really happens.

In the Bible, after Jesus is resurrected from the dead, he comes to his disciples, one of whom is a former prostitute named Mary. And Jesus says to her, 'Do not hold on to me.' It's as if he's saying, let go. Let go of me, and of the past. I'm not here so we can all be what we once were, but because even though it feels like we are turning back to where we came from, we are still moving forward on the journey. This is not a reanimation story, it's a resurrection story. It's a call to continue forward, but not as we once were.

Perhaps in your own life you are facing the end of a season and the start of a new one. As Jesus said, I urge you, do not hold on to it. Do not hold on to what was, and instead, stand to embrace the next twist and turn. Look to what is next. That doesn't mean don't grieve what was, but don't let your grief have the last word, because what's next is...well, it's your future. Maybe this resonates with you personally, but I also have this sense that it is where we are as a community. We are on the precipice of new and exciting and growing, and my prayer is that we can embrace it with so very much grace."

Who was the first person to pray, to walk a labyrinth, to meditate, to go all woo? I doubt we'll ever know, but it was someone, and they wanted to connect with a someone/thing else. A sense they had of the something beyond their understanding, beyond their senses. And then, something powerful or moving or meaningful happened because they shared the experience. And then, these practices, these experiences, were adopted by communities of people aware of and bound by their hunger for that same connection. This hunger, awareness, seeking connection, it is a deep an essential part of what it means to be human in the Divine image and an essential part of what it means to be Missing Peace and loving with all our heart and soul.

The practice of walking the labyrinth invites us into that connection. Creating space and noticing. Inviting and trusting. Opening ourselves and our schedules to new meaning. Not perfect, for perfection is a kind of death with no new life or growth to be had, but instead possibility, transformation, messy pink-haired-mermaid kind of hope that magic might happen in the midst of it all. And that we might notice it. Sight, smell, breath, intention, feel, hope, not denying our real-life humanity, but engaging it deeply through all that has been lovingly provided to us by the divine and the world she has woven. This is how we understand loving God with our heart and soul. This is how we woo.

CHAPTER 4

O f course, there is more than one way to woo. There are innumerable traditions and practices drawing Divine and human closer. What might happen if we get quiet and allow ourselves to be led closer? If we could let go of the white-knuckled grip we have on our lives and just breathe for a moment? It's risky. It doesn't feel safe, especially if our trust, our faith, has been used against us or to manipulate us or others. And, if we dare to hope, to risk…might magic/woo/Spirit/hope happen?

An openly available and well-revered way is the simplicity of quiet. It sounds too easy, and yet it's so rare. Not necessarily the absence of sound, though that is lovely to the extent it is possible, but quiet as a posture. Quiet as an opportunity to separate our human-doing-ness from our human-being-ness. A chance to sit still and listen for the still, small voice of God, of self, of the place that overlaps. A permission slip that says it's not only okay, but good to do so.

In addition to hosting a brief moment of silence each week, about once per year, Missing Peace hosts an event inspired by thebigquiet.com that's all about being quiet…together. We often do so around busy holiday seasons for a moment of respite from the go. At one of our favorite spots, the Bailey Riverbridge House, we are flanked on one side by the river and surrounded by beautiful gardens. The building has a wraparound porch, wood paneled floors and walls and is wide-open inside. It's long ago history as a Primitive Baptist Church gives it a certain feeling, a certain knowing that it is sacred space. It even still has a nostalgic church-y kind of smell…a little bit musty, a dab of pine cleaner and a hint of sweetness that brings back visceral memories.

As light streams in through the tall picture frame windows, we find a spot in the space to get comfortable. A chair, the floor, wherever stillness can best find us. A few words are gently offered to start us on our way, and then we simply sit together in the quiet. There is no closing, no benediction. People just gingerly leave when they are through. In this way, we leave space for the inspiration of Spirit—both in what happens in those still and quiet moments, but also when it is done, that it might go with us.

Sermon from quiet experience:

Calm in the Chaos

https://youtu.be/yqfgqSm9BUY

"In the face of tragedy, hardship, injustice, the first place we go is 'why?' Why has this happened? How could this happen? And there are voices out there loudly offering unsatisfying answers. Everything happens for a reason they'll tell me. Or even worse, in my opinion, if you just believed enough, had enough faith, then you'd have everything you want and nothing bad would happen. Or most disgusting to me, it's punishment…whatever bad storm or event or tragedy is a divine spanking for all our wrong-doing. In the midst of chaos, people want answers. When things feel out of control, people want reasons, answers, equations for how these things work so that we can somehow prevent them or protect ourselves.

But for me, these overly simplified, cosmic equations just aren't good enough. Don't tell me everything happens for a reason when my 6-year-old cousin is diagnosed with Leukemia. It's not good enough. And certainly, don't tell me that lack of faith is the reason people are going hungry in the richest country in the world. And if you dare venture into some kind of punishment explanation for why Houston is underwater or Irma took lives, not only is it not good enough, it's infuriating! These kinds of questions and the utterly unsatisfying answers only serve to drag us further into the chaos that made us ask them in the first place.

So, what's the alternative? There's an ancient rabbi you've probably heard of that aptly modeled another way. There's a story where he and his friends are out to sea in a boat, and this big storm rolls up. And despite being experienced fishermen and sailors, this storm is enough to shake them up and scare the crap out of them. And their friend, their teacher, this radical rabbi they've been hanging around with, is explaining why God does this to people and the reasons they're being punished and warns them they haven't been praying big enough. No. None of that. The truth is, he's sleeping in the boat. They're running around, freaking out, and Jesus is sleeping. So, they frantically wake him and beg him to do something, that they're all going to die if he doesn't. So, he wakes up and says 'peace, be still.' And soon the storm dies down, and the disciples calm down too.

Most often this is interpreted as Jesus' divine power over even mother nature; in fact, the disciples, his friends and students, seem to interpret it that way. But let me offer a different takeaway: What if it's not a miraculous display of God's powers to make a storm stop mid-rage, but instead is a call to us to hold on to our peace, to stay calm in the midst of chaos, because it never lasts and we can be so much more, learn so much more, if we can hold on to a little peace in the thick of it? May I further offer that it is the most chaotic moments in our lives that are the most formative. They show us who we are and invite us into who we want to be. And if we can keep our heads, if we can tap into a bit of the quiet hum at the source of it all, if we can listen to the call for 'peace, be still,' might there be even more life, meaning, hope, love, possibility and peace...even when the winds blow and the waters rise and everything that mattered is lost, and hope...even hope seems impossible?

Regardless of if you are in that place right now, or if you know someone who is, or if you have ever been in the swirling vortex of chaos and despair, today, we invite you into some peaceful space. Not just this building, but the peaceful space inside yourself, inherited from your divine heritage, and a part of you all along, the hum inside you that comes from the source of all creation and that is heard most clearly when we are quiet. Friends...peace, be still."

We then sat in our little rented space, in the quiet, until folks decided to start wandering off in ones and twos. We held that space for one another, honoring that there is more to us than what we can say or what we can do. Honoring that there is a deep wisdom in each of us and the value in making time to listen to it. Honoring that we need the "stop" at least as much as we need the "go." Honoring the woo.

Stillness, it's so very rare in our culture. It's seen as unproductive and written off as unimportant. Any action that doesn't qualify by the worldly standards of productivity or lead to the accumulation of things is seen as useless. The spiritual practices of Missing Peace beg to differ. Instead, we curate space that is intentionally for what the world calls "useless." Space that invites a consideration of value that has nothing to do with productivity. Space that is anti-efficient. Set apart, holy space.

These, and many more, are the ways in which we love God with our heart and soul. We cannot manufacture the experience of God, just as we cannot manufacture love, but we can hold the space and enter into it with hope. We can tune in with the parts of ourselves that cannot be measured, but somehow make up what is really and truly, and more than anything else, you. Something that's not connected to your achievements. Something that's not connected to your parents, children or spouse. Something that isn't gathered like information or moved like a body or completed like a task. Something that is purely, essentially and deeply you. And when we tune in that way, we often find divinity there. We find our maker, our divine Mother/Father. We find peace.

Loving With Heart and Soul Questions:

1. What are the moments in which you feel connected and at peace?

2. Are there practices that make you feel close to the Divine?

3. When do you feel grounded?

4. What ideas do you have to worship/love God with your spirit (heart and soul)?

Part 3:

WHAT ARE YOU THINKING? – LOVING WITH OUR MIND

But first, a story...

My longtime friend, Dr. Ashley Lear, teaches humanities through science fiction among other mediums at a local university. She is one of the "Mom Quad," with whom I first dreamed of Missing Peace and is active in a local church as an elder. This unique and interesting human wraps her arms around the vast experience of literature, video games, human experience and faith with abundant thoughtfulness and grace. She was a natural coconspirator as we developed Missing Peace.

In the midst of her teaching and research, one of Ashley's students pointed out that a character was being gaslit in the midst of the story progression. It started an adventure into learning more about gaslighting and brainwashing through the literature she and her class were studying. In her love of learning, Ashley couldn't help but share all that she was learning about these topics—how brainwashing is a large-scale shift, such as one might see in a cult, convincing the populous of an idea, and the much more intimate nature of gaslighting where an individual is convinced of a new reality in the confines of a relationship with a power disparity. As Ashely shared these insights, I couldn't help but see that this is how many in the unchurched and dechurched community feel about church, scripture and even God.

Ashley and I both became excited about creating a cerebral expression for Missing Peace overlapping what she was learning in academia and the stories of Christianity. With the view of church as a potential brainwasher, the characters of scripture falling into gaslighting and brainwashing scenarios and the tendency of the church to ignore things that make it uncomfortable, it felt like a cocktail for a meaningful, faithful and lively discussion.

Refusing to shy away from the tough topics, we put the word out that Missing Peace would host "Brainwashing, Gaslighting and Religion." We announced that all are welcome and so are their ideas. We created a unique space for people to process how they feel about these tendencies of religion through conversation and discussion with an expert.

CHAPTER 5

In many of the Missing Peace people's experiences of church, there was good entertainment, but it lacked, in one woman's terms, "the meat." There were well-produced visual and auditory experiences, complete with large bands, trained singers, smoke machines and lights. All the trappings of a well-produced concert, but when it came time for some thoughtful, meaningful and just conversation, it fell flat.

In other scenarios, they reported experiences of stiff pews, ancient music (poorly produced) and a message that was just soft. These spaces held nostalgia but didn't offer growth and engagement. It was like a trip back in time, not an opportunity to develop where they were in the present. The language, the people, the building itself all seemed to be holding on to some idyllic, even fictional, past.

In both of these options, the church created and presented something. The people were the audience, the consumer of the church-produced program/concert/message. Missing Peacers seemed to long for something else. They wanted to look at current issues, ask tough questions, engage the gospel and the news; they wanted to love God with all their mind. Likely, none of them would say it that way, but it was clear that dynamic, intellectual engagement was largely missing from the worship experience—and their life experience, for that matter—and they longed for it.

As a community, we wanted to compare and contrast what scripture taught us about the beginning of the creation and what science taught us about it too. We wanted to ask the tough questions that had been grading on our church connections and theology for so long. We wanted to dig into the scriptures and discern what's baby and what's bathwater—since so many had thrown out both. We wanted to enter our internal board rooms, explore the enneagram and host civil conversations. We valued that classic literature, science fiction and poetry could all invite us into a deeper intellectual relationship with God—or for those whom this language isn't accessible, with the bigger thing going on here.

One way to do this is through a program by NPR's Krista Tippet called *The Civil Conversations Project*: "Speaking together differently in order to live together differently."[iv] They offer a set of guidelines and virtues of these gatherings to help facilitate challenging conversations with civility. We utilized their format to host an open conversation around the news of the day. In our case, recent riots in Charlottesville and Boston.

We invited a university professor who is trained and experienced in facilitating challenging conversations. She is also an atheist, and we felt that credential (in addition to her others) would help curate an accessible and invitational space to people across the belief spectrum to share their thoughts and ideas.

We set up tables in a large square in our rented city space so that we might all face each other and be as equals at the table. I set the stage with a brief sermon, and our facilitator shared a little bit of her experience and some suggested ground rules for a civil conversation. We made space to create any additional guidelines the group thought would help us open up to honest and meaningful discussion, saying explicitly that if things got heated, we would consciously hold space to breathe so that we might maintain and honor the space we hoped to create.

Feeling we'd done all we could to honor the civil and honest space for the conversation, we dove in. Words and opinions came slowly at first, a bit awkwardly. People all wanted to be nice and just agree or say nothing, but soon, it became clear that we could, in fact, disagree and still be in the same space, still be kind, still even like each other while holding different opinions. Looking into each other's eyes, seeing the humanity of the people we were agreeing or disagreeing with made it possible to consciously choose our words to both be true and kind. We could honor each other without reducing an individual to the false dichotomies of democrat or republican, atheist or believer, right or wrong, in or out. It's easy in a space like that to see that people are far more complex creatures than any one issue they are for or against.

Sermon from Civil Conversations

Civil Conversations

https://youtu.be/xK-507cIyVA

"Interestingly, we chose Civil Conversations as a theme for this week long before Charlottesville and Boston and others were on your newsfeed. It was chosen because there are tensions rising in our country between races, between political parties, between police and African Americans, between religions—and somehow, governments and religions. And to be real honest about it, I want to hide from it most of the time. I want to take my kids to the beach and organize my garage and do my job and pretend everything is okay, or not as bad as this side or that side is making it out to be.

But I realize that is a rather cowardly response. And when people's lives and civil liberties and humanity are at stake, it is too important to put my head in the sand. That said, inflammatory tweets and posts...the verbal grenade tossing and withdraw enabled by social media...will rarely, if ever, change anyone's mind. It's like we all have access to these global microphones, but I have to wonder if any wisdom will rise above the cacophony of anger and hatred and memes that question my beliefs if I don't type amen and share.

How will we ever grow and learn and transform—and each of us needs to—if we don't look into eyes that disagree with us and have a meaningful conversation, to hear the other side as much as we speak, to conduct ourselves with civility and grace that might, just might touch a heart in the way our shouty, inflamed, disenchanted, desperate, clawing at the door of different-but-the-same neighbor somewhere on the other side of nowhere, ever could.

We won't, we can't solve the world's problems by gathering today. But we can open our eyes instead of hiding from what scares us. We can deepen our understanding of "the other," whoever they are. We can arm ourselves with language and ideas and hope in a way that no militia ever will.

Our problems, this country's problems, are not new problems. Every time there is a powerful, dominant regime, this happens. Fear creeps in that maybe we are slipping, our grip on the controls might not be as strong as we thought, and more fearsome people are put in power to "protect us." And fingers are pointed at anyone we can call enemy so we have someone to put our fear upon and can pretend we are safe because we've discovered the bad guys.

But it never works. Because when fear takes hold, society unravels. When we are more focused on shoring up our walls, or protecting our bounty, or defending our spot on the global or national or societal totem, we forget to care about each other. We can't think of anything else but taking care of number one. We become paranoid and hopeless and desperate, and it's nearly inevitable when you've forgotten what your religion or your family or your country stood for in the first place.

And maybe, just maybe, a small band of hopeful people coming to the table, talking through who we want to be with grace and compassion and selflessness that we pledge to hold one another accountable to can, in fact, make a difference. Because just like our history warns us of the downfall that comes when fear drives, it also reminds us to "never doubt that a small group of thoughtful, committed citizens can change the world. Indeed, it's the only thing that ever has." (Margaret Meade)

So, today we talk. We get a little uncomfortable, but we also commit to be understanding and to listening above all else."

We wanted to create safe, civil place to talk about the confusing and complicated issues plaguing us. And not in the over-confident, I've-got-a-side-and-it-is-bullet-proof kind of way that is so common in our society. Instead, we wanted a space that could listen well, and maybe we would actually learn something from one another instead of just getting louder and more certain with our own stance.

And so, we sat around a table together. People shared their hearts. We moderated the conversation that all might have a voice—those with quick tongues and those who prefer to ponder. We didn't come up with answers and action plans but formed our hearts through meaningful community connection and conversation.

At the risk of offense, and with the pressure of presenting a finished product, the church seems to have largely withdrawn from talking about tough issues. We'd rather say nothing than say the wrong thing. And what if we lose people by taking a stance? With dwindling attendance, each someone's attendance (and, if we're honest, tithe) makes a big difference…maybe the difference between life and death, of the church anyway. But that can cause poor decisions to be made when functioning out of the fear of life and death. And further, the gospel is a radical story of counter cultural love, inclusion and standing up to injustice. It certainly isn't about nice, tame messages crafted not to offend. So much so that the gospel's main character is killed for his beliefs and vocal and active preaching, teaching, and living of them. If we can't live that out as the church, what do we have left? No wonder they are leaving in droves.

We need to be able to clearly articulate what we believe, and then for that to match who we are. This is the biggest disconnect I've heard from people leaving the church. It's often called hypocrisy and sets people's bullshit meters off immediately. This is not, as some church folks will throw their hands up and quit over, a demand to be perfect from those outside the church. But it is a call to live into what you say you believe and to be forthright about it, even if it kills the church, because we're supposed to be the ones that believe in resurrection.

CHAPTER 6

Often, our cerebral engagements will have this conversational character. One of the major elements we feel is missing from many traditional worship services, is interactivity of the gathered people. A chance to contribute, question, engage with what is being presented. When we hear from more voices, we get a broader view, more information and a widening of each one's lens.

Poetry, with its gracious interpretation of life, has been a useful entry point into conversations like this. It often will capture, not unlike scripture, the heart of a thing. The literal or factual is able to be set aside to get at the deeper thing going on. The deeper sense of our united humanity, a deeper sense of the "in all" and "through all" things (Ephesians 4:6) that we are invited into in the universal Christ. Some things are so real and so true, that the factual articulation of them fails to capture them at all. In these places, metaphor and parable serve much better—much like Jesus used to teach about the kingdom of God.

Whether it's the Psalms or Mary Oliver, all of us have felt the movement of Spirit in the reading and hearing of poetry. By exploring it in community, we have the opportunity to dig in deeply to what God is up to in the world. How we understand spiritual concepts that fail to be captured in other ways. An inroad to how we think about God, relate to God, through metaphor and image and word pictures.

For one such gathering, our nomadic group met at a small neighborhood clubhouse. There were children all over the room playing and jabbering in that special brand of kid talk. It was a hot, late summer day, and we relished the cool interior of the borrowed space. We made do with a long, wooden conference table and some open floor space (for all that running around). There were no sound systems, no music, no fancy light. Just a small group of humans, some moving ideas and lots of good conversation.

Sermon from our poetry exploration

Poetry, Faith and Geese

https://youtu.be/vfVPzkkDyhM

Wild Geese by Mary Oliver

You do not have to be good.

You do not have to walk on your knees

For a hundred miles through the desert, repenting.

You only have to let the soft animal of your body

love what it loves.

Tell me about your despair, yours, and I will tell you mine.

Meanwhile the world goes on.

Meanwhile the sun and the clear pebbles of the rain

are moving across the landscapes,

over the prairies and the deep trees,

the mountains and the rivers.

Meanwhile the wild geese, high in the clean blue air,

are heading home again.

Whoever you are, no matter how lonely,

the world offers itself to your imagination,

calls to you like the wild geese, harsh and exciting—

over and over announcing your place

in the family of things.

"*I love this poem. The way Mary Oliver has crafted these words together in this beautiful tapestry. The way each line on its own might just be a pretty thread but woven together with the loom of her pen creates this beautiful landscape. It creates this layered world with its own topography, and each of us settles on a different peak, valley or plain. Each of us looks at this work and sifts out a meaning that seems somehow crafted just for me.*

For me, this poem is a great exhale. It's this sigh of relief. You don't have to be good...what a relief because I am not...not really. There are times in life when you or I walk around with a smile plastered on our faces that just barely masks the darkness within. Knowing this keeps us in this defensive state where we are constantly trying to prove ourselves. Perhaps I should just speak for myself here, but I'm fairly confident this isn't just true of me. I see evidence of it all over our nation and our world... each country or corporation or individual climbing over the backs of the one before it, all clamoring to stake our claim and prove our value. And each time we reach some kind of benchmark or goal, finding ourselves unfulfilled even still, and barely even taking a breath before we begin clamoring once again. But here, Mary Oliver reminds us there is another choice. We don't have to be part of that game. 'You do not have to be good... you don't have to crawl through the desert repenting...' There is another option.

Interestingly, this poem resonates this week's scripture from Mark where the disciples and Jesus are on a journey. It's kinda their thing. But along the way, they start to argue about being good. In fact, about being the best. They begin to play that clamoring game of one-upmanship...who is the best? Who has the most to offer to the group? Scripture doesn't share the content of this argument, but surely they were boasting over who was the smartest, or who had given the most or who had done the most service projects? What a shame, huh? Even the seemingly good deeds being used to say who is better than who.

So, anyway, Jesus notices his students arguing. And, as he's wont to do, he asks 'what were you arguing about?' I'm guessing teachers can identify with this…they get all quiet on him. Like, super-guilty-quiet on him. What he likely already knows is they were arguing about who had walked on their knees a hundred miles through the desert, if you know what I mean. They were arguing about who was the greatest disciple… So, I'm sure Jesus was way more patient than me, but I imagine one big ol' eye roll from Jesus here. Seriously guys? Have you not figured this out at all? By the way, the gospels are always answering that with a resounding no.

They don't get it…So, Jesus gets all radical reversal on them…again, as he is wont to do. And he says, 'just let the soft animal of your body love what it loves.' Wait, that's not it…but it's not too far off when you think about it. 'Whoever wants to be the first must be the last and servant to all.' Whoever wants to be tough, like crawl-through-the-desert-tough, must be soft and gentle, whoever wants to be great must serve, whoever wants to be strong must be vulnerable.

And then, in case they still don't get it, he scoops up one of the children in his arms and tells them to love the kids…and by doing so, that's how you love God. By loving each other, by serving each other, by being vulnerable and living out of a place of love instead of fear, that's how you live according to Jesus' teachings. That's how we live a life of peace. We don't live into the despair of me or of you…we live into the harmony of earth where the world goes on and the rain still falls, and the wild geese make their annual pilgrimage above our heads.

Now, don't get me wrong here. That doesn't mean ignore or attempt to eliminate your fear or despair or doubt…I don't think that's possible…but for heaven's sake, don't let it drive. Keep it in the back seat. It can be a good warning and a healthy part of your complete self, but the second fear and doubt and despair take the wheel, we find ourselves on that treadmill of clawing to justify our existence. We find ourselves on our knees in that desert.

And yet, that sneaky force of destruction, fear and doubt, will sometimes find its way into our driver's seat…it happens to all of us…those dark cloud days or the days where we feel worthless or hopeless…in those days, remember the sound of the wild geese 'harsh and exciting, over and over announcing your place in the family of things.'

You belong, and you belong, and you belong…each of you belong in this world, and I believe, in this place, in this time. You have a place here, and you don't have to crawl through the desert to justify it. You don't have to argue for your place in it…you belong here. You are on purpose.

I believe, most days confidently, in this loving creator God who made me, on purpose, and that I belong. And every day, I try to make sure my children know that same thing. You are on purpose, my beloved child; you belong. They don't have to fight for my love or prove themselves or bring anything to the table except to be authentically them…and, my GOD, how I love them. From the depths of my being, I love those two little girls, more than I ever knew was possible. And somehow, that makes me understand why God would love me and want me. Flawed, broken, doubtful, cynical me. Not because of what we do or who is the greatest, but because we are God's children, and we are beloved.

Listen, I know what I'm telling you isn't logical. Stephen Colbert recently said, 'Logic will not finally lead me to God, but my love and gratitude for God's work in creation can.' 'Meanwhile the sun and the clear pebbles of the rain are moving across the landscapes, over the prairies and the deep trees, the mountains and the rivers. Meanwhile the wild geese, high in the clean blue air, are heading home again. Whoever you are, no matter how lonely, the world offers itself to your imagination, calls to you like the wild geese, harsh and exciting — over and over announcing your place in the family of things.' May you hear God's voice and see in God's work that you are beloved and on purpose, and you belong. Amen."

After this sermon, a local professor, friend and poet, Jessica Kester (also of MomQuad fame), helped lead us in a discussion on exploration of poetry. We looked through poems together, highlighted the parts that jumped out and shared what we understood them to mean. We found imagination, creativity, life lessons, and often, a personal word through the medium of poetry.

Engaging our intellect, and doing it in a deep and interactive way, has made space for the transformation we are so hopeful to see. Our most outspoken atheist recounts these kinds of experiences as being some of the most meaningful for him, despite initial reluctance or concerns of indoctrination efforts. Instead, he found a place where his ideas and input are valued, and he could both be heard and hear. And that is holy.

People are hungry for deep, meaningful and intellectual conversations. Interactions where we don't have to demean another in order that we might have something valuable to say. Spaces where all are honored as children of God, made in the divine image, and their thoughts and ideas create space for each to learn and grow, and perhaps most importantly, fertile ground for meaningful relationship to the Holy and to the holy in each of us.

This is why we "love God with our mind" as the scriptures beckon. That we might use the great gift of our intellect in contrast to, but not to the exclusion of, taking it on faith. This God we worship, this faith we have, can stand up to our scrutiny and questioning. The danger of exploring deeply with our minds is low, but the reward is great...if we can but quell our fear and be vulnerable together.

Loving With Mind Questions:

1. How do you meet God in the midst of your thinking critically?

2. Where do you spot God in the midst of scientific understandings or methods?

3. What are you reading that compels you to deeper understanding or connection?

4. What are the conversations or questions you're longing to dig into deeper?

Part 4:

WALK IT OUT –
LOVING OTHERS AS SELF

But first, a story...

Early in the formation of Missing Peace, I had a conversation with some of the leadership at First Presbyterian Church of Daytona Beach. They were moved by my passion for this project and wanted to be supportive in their prayer, partnership and financial support.

On campus at First Daytona, they had a community garden in need of some love, and I saw an opportunity. I would bring the Missing Peace community to them on one of our serving Sundays and help clean up the garden. I painted a picture of all these young families, a demographic they longed for, coming to their church. I asked them to send some of their leaders to meet our people. I dreamed with them about all the potent metaphor in gardens and what a great project and transformation opportunity this could be – both in the individual and on their campus.

As we approached this gardening Sunday project, excitement was high. I called ahead and confirmed space, people, times, etc. I gushed about the families that would come and help. I gathered supplies, advertised on social media and told every person I knew. I worked all week on just the perfect words to frame this already-potent metaphor in the garden. All the pieces were in place for a massive, transformational, God-infused, partnership-cementing, amazing experience.

That Sunday came. The weather was right. Our hosts were ready. The space was set. My family and I showed up early with signage and supplies to make sure the experience would be awesome for all involved. And we waited for the hordes to arrive. And then we waited some more. Then our hosts began to ask where all these young families were. Soon, my little family and I realized, it was just us.

I gave a half-assed version of my sermon to my family, and we went and weeded for about an hour, then we left. The floodgates of my broken heart fell open. I questioned this calling, I questioned God, I questioned humanity. I wanted to quit…everything.

In that moment, my husband, a reluctant supporter to this point, looked in my bloodshot and over running eyes and said, "You can't quit, Katy. I've never believed more than now how important this work is. The world needs this. I need this. Please keep going."

The shards of my heart and my call became a little stronger in that moment. I was by no means healed, but this imperfect work, this wild and creative and heart-opening work would not end on that Sunday nearly five years ago. It would teach me that failure is an intimate partner of creative experiment.

CHAPTER 7

One of the pieces that is essential to Missing Peace is living into the claims we make and doing it together. Living out who we say we are as an act of worship. This is where the word becomes flesh. This is where our most potent weapon against hypocrisy comes in to play. "We will be who we say we are" is just as important a piece as "we will learn and develop who we are." We will live out the things we claim just as readily as we discuss them. We will love our neighbors through real, hands-on serving. This is how we be Missing Peace. This is how we be church.

Because we are already nomadic in nature, it makes executing this idea easier than for a traditional gathering in a consistent space. We are agile enough to gather on Sundays where the help is needed—beaches, shelters, assisted living facilities, etc. That said, our efforts have influenced a local church to begin a serving week once per quarter. They have an abbreviated worship service, then do a project either for the church or a partner organization. In this way they are actively being the hands and feet of Christ—together. This leads me to believe that worship through serving, aka loving neighbor as self, is possible in any context.

For Missing Peace, our serving weeks have become one of the most popular and meaningful ways that we gather. That said, we have been careful about not over-emphasizing this piece. It would be easy to put the emphasis on the doing, it's our cultural norm, but we are also deeply focused on the being. We need the right fuel, we need the connectional pieces, to add meaning to our effort. An effort we hope is formative to the participants and recipients of the love we are sharing, shaping us into the likeness of our divine parentage.

For one of our service opportunities, we partnered with an organization called ARC of Volusia who has the mission of "Providing the opportunity for hope, growth and change to people with intellectual and developmental disabilities in our community."ᵛ One of our Missing Peacers has a huge heart for this population after growing up around people with these kinds of disabilities. She helped organize an opportunity for us to serve this community by rejuvenating a garden they work in, creating notes and pictures, and cleaning up a walking trail on campus. In addition, we met some of the staff and clients of ARC and were moved by their stories of hope.

You probably won't be surprised, based on our Florida location, that when we gathered at ARC, it was hot. And I mean, take your breath away, drench your shirt, water-gulping kind of hot. And our project was largely outside on the campus. We met at 10:30 in the morning, and it only got hotter as we went on. The cicadas taunted us from surrounding bushes, seeming to beckon the sun even higher in the sky. Thank God for an occasional breeze and some shade from the trees.

The garden at ARC was only about 10ft. X 10ft. but was so inundated with weeds that it seemed much larger to the naked eye. But we were here, and we'd committed, so we dove in. Sweating it out, a few began inching their way through the weed-tangled garden, while others began cutting back an overgrown path that wound through the campus. My anxious leader's heart relaxed as conversation and laughter seemed to ward off the sun's efforts to bake us.

When the work was as done as we could get it, we gathered inside the ARC building to recover and reflect. The maintenance man and grounds keeper shared with us through strained voice and tear-filled eyes what it meant to have people invest in this disregarded group of folks, and how much they've come to mean to him over the years. Our sweaty but happy crew thanked him for the chance to be a small part of that.

Sermon from ARC of Volusia week:

Getting Comfortable?

https://youtu.be/PClxAyzgu0Y

"It's been a while, but we used to say quite often at Missing Peace, 'You should never be more than 75% comfortable with what happens here…the 25% is where you'll learn and grow.' As we come up to our third anniversary next month, I wonder if we haven't gotten a bit comfortable. If you're here for the first time, or don't attend with great frequency, it may not be true for you, but for me and for many of our regulars, we've sort of settled in. Have we not? We see many of the same faces, we've got habits of checking texts or Facebook to know where to go and what to bring, the liturgies or rituals have become norms to many of us. While from the outside looking in we remain way outside the box, for some of us, it's… well… comfortable, predictable… ours.

So, what? You might say. What difference does it make? Why does it matter if we, who have felt outside the scope of religion for so long, begin to feel less so? On one hand, that's good news. After all, our mission is to create space for diverse believers to participate in their spiritual evolution. So, good. Huzzah! And I also know the stories of outside the box, Jewish revolutionaries who were focused on doing good, being good, helping others and tying it all together with a shared meal to remember who and what and why they are. But somehow, all those good intentions and outside-the-box thinking led to Christendom, organized religion, rigidity…the very boxes they were originally way outside of.

It's only natural that individuals and organizations grow up. And as they do, certain things solidify a bit…stop growing and changing. It's part of the circle of life. It makes us feel safer and more secure when things are predictable, more solid. However, solid also often means brittle and fragile...it's often a false security. But if we can instead remain flexible and adaptable...that's the counter-intuitive and yet far more reliable and secure posture. It's true for our bodies; pliable, flexible bodies are less prone to injury. It's true for raising our children; harsh, rigid structures don't create the space for kids to discover themselves. It's true for our institutions...when they become overly-hardened they begin to crumble. It's true for relationships...if we cling too tightly, they fall apart. And it's true for ourselves; if we aren't gracious and gentle with ourselves, we too begin to crumble and fall apart.

And so, I hope this and all of our Missing Peace experiences make you a little uncomfortable. I hope they stretch you a bit...get you outside of your comfort zone. I hope that it makes us question who and why and what we are. I hope that it begs cosmic, universal questions of justice and fairness, openness and inclusiveness. Not because we will come up with solid answers or remedies, but because when we are questioning, when we are looking into the face of that which we don't fully understand, we are participating in our evolution, our continued becoming. We are creating empathy and working our compassion muscles. We are stretching ourselves in hopes of staying spiritually, mentally and physically pliable that we may not become complacent and rigid and stuck in who we think we are but may continually live into the divine spark inside each of us and in each we meet. That we might be stretched and flexible and increasingly open and inclusive and living out of and into love."

After this sermon and hearing some of the first-hand experiences of clients and staff, we were invigorated and wanted to do something immediately to serve. Gathering in this way creates the opportunity to act on that impulse and put our hearts and flesh into action, loving our neighbor. Thus, creating that incarnational, transformative space we long for more of in our lives.

In addition to our efforts to be incarnational, we also want to be responsive to what is happening in the real world. We don't want to get into a rhythm of saying, "I've done my part" or "I'm not part of the problem" and thus ignoring any role we could take in our larger community or country. And so, we serve and also speak to the issues of our time. Because if we don't, who will? "Christ has no hands and feet on this earth but ours,"[vi] as Teresa Avila reminds us.

CHAPTER 8

Aservice concept we have revisited a number of times is taking time to be with underserved populations in our community. Here in Florida, that is clearly exampled in our large elderly population. While medical efforts help keep folks alive and well much longer than ever, they don't always account for the larger things that make us human. Our heart, spirit, the intangible things our deepest essence is made of are often neglected for underserved populations, just as they are in the wider population. We relish the chance for us and our kids to spend time with these people who have lived long lives, who've experienced much and who value the connection of just being together in a way most of our busy lives don't allow for.

Countryside Lakes is located in Port Orange, FL. It's a bit of a hike (20 minutes down I-95) from most of Missing Peace's usual haunts. But we had a connection through a friend who teaches yoga there, and they were receptive to our desire to visit. Pulling up to the facility, we noticed well-kept grounds and modern architecture, making for an overall welcoming and pleasing introduction to the venue. As we gathered, we were invited in and told of the nightly happy hour with beer on tap and swimming pool out back. Charmed, many of us asked about reserving our own spot and if there was an age requirement.

It was nearing brunch time, and our plan was to go into the dining room to visit with the residents. Our kids sat and made little crafts while I gave a brief talk, and then we were invited down a little hallway, through some doors and into a sunny room with bright walls and chatting people at a collection of tables. At first, we were a bit timid. "What do we do?" But the kids knew. They immediately went and began delivering their freshly-made gifts. The delight on the faces of grateful recipients strengthened the rest of us to start a conversation, ask "Is it okay if I join you for a bit?" and ingratiate ourselves with these elderly folks gathered at tables.

A sermon from serving Countryside Lakes

Compassion Fatigue

https://youtu.be/U7yoMSr_hso

"Each time we partner with an organization on a serving week, we ask what we can do to help and to serve their organization. We also give our monthly community tithe to the organization to further that mission. And last, but definitely not least, we ask to hear about the mission and the people it serves from those actively involved. They bring the human story of these selfless endeavors in a way we could never capture on our own. And it is inevitably a huge gift to us to grow and learn through these partnerships.

Once again, it seems like a nearly endless stream. We are in the midst of a highly visible national moral crisis. I'm, of course, talking about what's going on at the border—families separated, people seeking asylum and hope, are being increasingly criminalized. And this is not the total fault of one administration or political party but is, in fact, much further reaching than that. There is a national hardening of hearts that is happening. Partly out of compassion fatigue—social media and 24-hour news networks have made it all too easy to become overwhelmed by all the disasters of the world...natural, emotional, manmade, etc., etc., etc—and partly symptomatic of a fear that if we don't fiercely guard our American way, it will be gone.

So, what do we do with it all? How do we process, respond, transform in the light of our changing world? How do we not become paralyzed but finetune our filters that we might pay attention and respond to what's most important and let the rest go? Here are five simple steps to respond in tumultuous times.

I'm kidding. It's not that simple. There are no 5 simple steps, and the efforts of so many to boil it down and make it more understandable are peeling away important nuances that help us remain sympathetic but also empowered. Each of these issues is far more complex than yes and no and who deserves what and what is legal and illegal. It's just not that simple. We're just not in the shoes of the other—whoever that other is...governmental power, border-dwelling U.S. residents, the immigrant population, the refugee...

Well, here's one thing we can do. We can foster empathy. We can continually push ourselves to know and relate with those who are different and broaden our take on frustratingly complex politically weighty issues. And by doing so, perhaps we can remain the calm, non-anxious voice of reason in the midst of bifurcated, overly confident, dualistic battles over right and wrong.

As a faith leader, I feel a strong need to respond to the way scripture was used to justify some of the recent political choices made. I know I have a Facebook friend list far more heavily-weighted with pastors than most, and so feel confident in saying there's been a loud and frustrated backlash of biblical scholars at any interpretation of this text that justifies separating families from each other or even the poor treatment of refugee/immigrant/U.S. hopefuls as a whole. One of the loudest messages of these ancient religious texts, old testament and new, is love your neighbor...is make space for the alien among you....is filled with cautions of treating people with dignity and respect in large part because it was written by a people who were enslaved for generations. Don't forget that you were once slaves in Egypt. You're free now. Treat others with the love and respect you once could only dream of. This is one of the most prevalent messages of scripture.[vii] And the stories and verses that fly in the face of this call are often there as tales of warning when people have faltered in this essential core value.

Here's the thing. When we dehumanize others, we erode ourselves and what it essentially means to be human. When we say this person counts for less because they are Black, we dehumanize ourselves. When we say this person doesn't matter because they aren't a U.S. citizen, we dehumanize ourselves. When we say this person is old and losing it, so they don't need the same things I need like friendship and laughter and good food and fun, then we are dehumanizing ourselves and all that it means to be created in the Divine image, to be children of the Divine, to be harborers of the Divine spark...a soul...a truest, deepest essence that knows who we are at our best.

So, if you weren't sure, that's what we're here for today. To nurture and maintain our compassion and empathy in tangible ways with real, witnessed effects that we might not become exhausted and hopeless in the larger context of all that is wrong in the world. We are exercising our empathy muscles in effective ways, and we're nurturing that deepest sense of self, the divine image, that truest most essential part of us that connects all life and beyond because that's the people we want to be, and the rest of our world offers very little opportunity to do that in constructive ways.

So, we'll be different. And we'll connect and inspire and enjoy and nurture our oft neglected and tired souls...and minister to the other and each other while we do. Amen."

We believe that service is not just a way to love our neighbors but also to love ourselves. All involved benefit when we reach out, connect and offer our gifts. We are transformed, hearts are softened, views are widened. Suddenly, there is space where there was no space, possibility where there was no possibility. Our compassion muscles are grown that we might not become so fatigued by the nearly constant draws on them.

There's something that resonates deep within us when we serve. Perhaps that's why it's so frequently heralded in scripture. But in many churches, we've made this a secondary mission with worship being primary. At Missing Peace, we insist that it can be both. We look to why we do these acts—our motivation, the scriptures, the need we see in the world that generate meaningful discussion and sermon fodder—as we look to love others as we love ourselves. By encountering the intersection of the world's great need and our great gifts, we identify our calling. And by living in our calling, we honor our divine image and connect with God and each other in meaningful ways. This is not just mission or service; this is worship.

As the time came to leave Countryside Lakes, our once timid group didn't want to go. Relationships had begun to form, stories were being told, sparkly pipe cleaner bracelets were being worn. It began to feel more like family than the oft-neglected elderly of our community we had come to serve. They weren't the recipients of our efforts; they were becoming our friends.

Loving Others as Self Questions:

1. What does serving have to do with being human?

2. Where do you see the deepest need in your community?

3. What are the ways you feel called to address that need?

4. What are your unique gifts? How might you use them for the good of the world?

Part 5:

FORM AND STRUCTURE

But first, a story...

As a nomadic community, we've learned to be very creative with the trappings of our time together. Candles, paraments, robes, stoles, pulpits—basically all the things that make up the setting of a traditional church service—aren't practical at the beaches, parks, city buildings, museums and homeless shelters where we worship.

One year, as we were approaching the liturgical season of Advent, we wanted to honor the tradition of the advent wreath and weekly candle lighting signifying the joy, love, peace and hope of the season, but it had to be portable.

So, I found a large glass bowl and filed it with small glass beads in which I could nestle the 4 weekly candles and the centered Christ candle to be lit on Christmas Eve. It was small enough to bring to our various venues and looked suitably sacred to mark the occasion.

For the first two weeks of Advent, it worked perfectly. We had a little reading, lit the candle and went on with our sacred gathering feeling appropriately festive and sacred for the holy season. But did I mention, it was glass?

While gathering up the supplies for the third week of Advent, it happened. A loud crack rang out from the bottom of a crate, and the sliding and clicking of glass beads scattering followed. I momentarily froze but quickly decided I could make this into an object lesson. I'll glue it back together, and the imperfection will show how things can both be broken and beautiful.

The next hour or so was full of language I don't care to include and a mound of frustration as I tried to force with advent wreath into an object lesson it seemed bent against. Nothing would hold together. The glue was inadequate for the task. The bowl didn't want to be rebuilt, and the start of our Missing Peace gathering was bearing down on me.

So, I scooped up the tattered remains, a few glass beads and the candles I could, and we rushed off to the park where we were meeting that week. The Advent wreath was no more. I scattered its parts on the sidewalk and couldn't even get candles lit in the gentle breeze of the day. *Christmas is ruined!* But it wasn't. Not really. That day, we hung scarves on trees for our neighbors experiencing homelessness, and it was all the holy we needed.

CHAPTER 9

As we extol the virtues of experiential worship, of the ways that God/Source/Universe is present in all that we are and do if we but pay attention, what (if any) place does liturgy have? Like I so often ask my kids of their words: Is it necessary? Is it helpful?

In the earliest gatherings of Missing Peace, we focused on the week's talk and the activity itself. This was good "meat" for the thing, but we found that we wanted ways to invite ourselves in. We wanted ways to set the stage for what we intended to do together. And we found that a lot of the traditional ways this had been done in church settings were off-putting for people.

So, once again, we took what was resonating with people in the world and overlaid it with traditional teachings and liturgies. We looked for where these things overlapped and differed. We looked at what it is about these words, rituals, prayers, etc. that resonated with people and why. And then, we did a lot of tweaking—we still are in many ways—to keep these pieces fresh and relevant.

Welcome

Whether it's your yoga class, your church service or a business meeting, there is always some kind of welcome. Some kind of inviting in and stating the intention for the time together. A brief statement of who we are, what we intend to do together this day and what's coming up. This helps us remember who we are, tells new folks who we are and keeps track of where we are headed.

Welcome to Missing Peace. We are a nomadic community seeking God through physical activities, cerebral engagements, spiritual practices and serving opportunities. Exploring how each of us experiences God makes us who we are, so please share your ideas with us. This week begins our Empathy Kids program with stories and activities crafted to build empathy in our kids. Next week we'll continue our mindful Labyrinth series at the Central Park labyrinth on Hammock Ln. The week after, we'll be checking back in with the Bahamas Relief effort and what is still needed there.

This piece functions much as it would in either a secular setting or a traditional church setting. It calls our gathering together. It keeps us informed. It begins to announce this time as unique from the rest of our lives and for a specific purpose.

Candle Lighting

The next invitation in our gathering we borrowed from a natural overlap we observed from both secular and spiritual settings. Whenever there was a tragedy in our community (local or national), people felt drawn together to mourn, vent or otherwise connect. This was often done through a candlelight vigil. It's as if the physical act of making light could ward off the felt darkness of the world, an event, a moment. This act is accessible to all kinds of people, no matter their beliefs, so it made sense in our effort at radical hospitality to invite people into a kind of prayer through candle lighting.

From a practical standpoint, we needed this act to be highly portable and functional in all kinds of spaces. So, we purchased small battery-powered candles that we could pass out to the participants so we could share in this communal act of making light in the world.

We also wanted to take this opportunity to invite another sense into the experience. We would call on the ancient practice of anointing and the current craze around essential oils and unite them during our candlelight moment. Yet another touch point announcing this time as set apart. The oil is passed with the candles, and those who desire can apply some as they feel moved to do so.

Candle Lighting Language

As this tray comes around, feel free to take some oil and a candle, and as you hold it, think about someone or something for which you'd like good thoughts, prayer or some hope. As something comes to mind, light your candle. If any would like to share with the group, please feel free. (Allow time and space for contributions and invite the gathered to hold these concerns for one another, saying: Would someone volunteer to hold this concern in prayer this week?) Let this light remind us of the light inside us all, the light of the world, a light that will never be overcome by darkness. May our prayers be heard, and we all be activated. Amen.

By inviting someone in the community to hold the prayer from another's heart, we share our burdens. The proverbial "a trouble shared is a trouble halved." If we share it with a whole community, what might happen? And so, we hold our concerns, and those of the world, together.

It's also an essential piece of our ethos that we talk about being active in our prayers. That we aren't simply offering these up and being helpless in the midst of them, but that we move and act in the ways we can. As Rabbi Abraham Joshua Heschel testified in the midst of the Civil Rights movement, "We must pray with our feet."[viii]

Breath Prayer

The candle lighting sets a more sacred tone in our space, which we continue with a breathing exercise. With the simple and essential act of breathing, we center ourselves and prepare our hearts for worshipful moments and heart forward space together.

Breath is not only an essential act, but often used in various physical practices to prepare the self, once again making it accessible as we attempt radical hospitality. It also has a whole host of scientific studies on how it effects our neurological, cardiovascular, limbic and other systems. And of course, it has Biblical connotations as it is commonly overlaid with Spirit in scripture.

Breath Prayer Language

Take a moment to focus your breath. Now, take a couple of slow, deep, cleansing breaths. In most of our life, we take these shallow breaths, just skimming the surface of our capacity. When we breathe deeply, we remember there is so much more that is possible. Similarly, we recognize that much of our life is just skimming the surface of our spiritual capacity in a beautiful sunset or perfect butterfly. But when we gather for Missing Peace, we breathe deeply and open ourselves to this time being different, set apart, holy time where we can deepen our spiritual experience. Focus on your breath, and let's spend a few moments in silence.

Breathing deeply and mindfully, silence, general slowing down, is all so rare in our lives, even more so doing these things in community. And so, we do them together each time we gather, announcing how this time is different from the everyday. Announcing our hope for something beyond the grind of so-called "normal life." Something I might call, the kingdom.

Community Statement

Very early on, we wanted a thoughtful announcement of who we are, why we gather and why it matters. This would be similar to an affirmation at a traditional service, or to reading the 12 steps at an AA meeting. We want to be as clear as we can with what we are about without stifling each one's uniqueness and, as ever, hold with great care and gentleness hospitality toward the unchurched, dechurched, alienated from church or otherwise suspicious. So, we carefully chose words that could both announce our intention but also leave space for a broad cross section of beliefs and spiritual journeys.

Community Statement Language

We are here as a community of families and friends gathered in response to an urging from beyond ourselves. We acknowledge that God (a name for the source of all good, love and peace attested to in the scriptures) is at work in this beautiful and broken world, and we are committed to joining in that work. We have found that, no matter how our life looks from the outside, whether we are Christian or agnostic, whether we are successful or struggling, whether we are confident or doubtful, or anywhere in between, we all need more peace. For that reason, we seek. We seek to know who we are in light of a God who loves us and this broken and fearful world. We seek to understand the message of Jesus meant not for Christianity but for all humanity. We seek the way, truth and life, partnered with the Spirit for the good of ourselves, our families, our community and our world.

Through these words, we claim our intention and identity as a community. Each person doesn't necessarily resonate with each word. For some, it's too specific and for others, too general, but we agree to operate under this statement as a community when in community.

Sermon

The next section of our gathering is targeted at placing the day's activity in the context of scripture and the world. In a brief 5-7 minutes, I'll craft a frame for the physical, spiritual, cerebral, or service activity of the day. There are examples of each in the previous chapters or on the Missing Peace Community YouTube channel.

During this time, we have an invitation for the children as well. Depending on the week's activity, this will vary some. If we are doing an activity that requires a lot of parental focus on the topic – this could be a very serene spiritual practice or a deep intellectual conversation –

we'll have age-appropriate programming for the kids. For example, we hosted an Empathy Kids program where we used children's stories paired with an activity to encourage empathy in our children. We've also hosted Recreative Arts where kids turned recycled items into advent calendars. In this way, we create a space for the kids to participate and the parents to focus.

On the weeks where we are doing service or physical activities, or any other kid-accessible programming, we invite them to stay present. They are addressed directly and given three options: "You may draw quietly, read quietly, or listen quietly," along with an assurance that I won't "talk too long." Each week, we provide appropriate art and reading materials for their use. Whatever the week's engagement, the kids are invited to stay present with the adults if they choose, and we trust parents to take the lead on what they think is best.

This portion is also where we would introduce any guest leadership. Sometimes this is a community member sharing why they requested the day's activity and how they experience the Divine through it. It could also be an outside expert helping to craft an engagement the community was interested in exploring. The latter has been the case for yoga, meditation, vocal experiences and others. In this way, we broaden our perspective by witnessing a variety of leadership.

Activity

Immediately following the sermon, we enter the day's physical, cerebral, spiritual or service experience. This is our response to the word. After talking about what we experience, believe, wonder about, we engage it in real time. This is an essential part of this incarnational effort at spiritual community, our version of church. For more, see previous chapters highlighting each type of activity.

Closing

In a traditional worship setting, there is a benediction or blessing. At the end of a class, a teacher might point out what was learned and what's coming next. At the end of an AA meeting, there is prayer and a closing reminder to "keep coming back." In the vein of each of these, we crafted a closing for Missing Peace that would function in these ways and be, as ever, accessible. We also wanted it to be interactive, as so much of our liturgy is. This creates the space to both share and cement learnings and takeaways from our time together.

Closing Language

Before we close, would anyone like to share a few words about today's experience? (Leave space for participants to share.) Thanks for being here today and sharing in this experience together. You so deserve it. May this experience kindle the light inside you and fuel the light of the world, a light that will never be overcome by the darkness. I want to invite you to repeat some closing words that represent what we are journeying together toward. "Do Justice, Love Kindness, and Walk Humbly." Hope you enjoy your mindful Sunday next week, and if you want ideas for that, check out Facebook. We'll be back together at Gold Leaf for a Bahamas check-in on 2/9 and again nourish our goodness, hope and light. Please take a moment to gift us a message in our guest book, or gift us financial support so we may keep gathering. Grace and Peace friends.

Each of these pieces is revisited and adjusted on an as-needed basis, often through surveying the gathered people for their thoughts and feelings about them. We are ever developing, and never static. And yet, these pieces also create a sense of consistency when so much of what Missing Peace does together is variable. It helps people know what to expect and hand-holds as we create this space together.

When it comes to liturgy, we've realized that there is great value in it. People like to know what to expect, like to have some things they can count on being part of their experience. And, at the same time, we believe they should be regularly edited, evaluated and open to change. We believe this about all the things we do together because we as a people are not stagnant and neither should be how we gather and connect with God and others – what Missing Peace calls worship.

Liturgy Questions:

1. What would it be like to translate traditional liturgy to more common/relatable language?

2. What are the liturgies of your life? What are the liturgies of your community?

3. Think about the point of different rituals and liturgies. Why do we do them? Might there be other ways to get at the point?

4. Look at your rituals and routines of daily life. Are there ways to pay attention to the holy in the midst of them? What is the point of them? (Drill down on this with multiple "whys.")

CHAPTER 10

We believe we are *the* church, even if we can't fully embrace the idea that we are *a* church. And as the church, we want to lend our voice to how we understand the holy days. Our culture has appropriated much of Christian holy days to be opportunities for exorbitance. We eat exorbitantly, we spend exorbitantly, and quietly, the hope-filled origin story of these holy days eeks out around the edges.

Christmas

It's not as simple as "keeping the Christ in Christmas," which has come to be understood as "the Christians own this holiday, now back off." Instead, it is calling us to the deep connectional story of humanity in the Divine image and what that means. A story of light in the darkness, a story of hope when all seems dead. That's a story that relates to all people and is counter-cultural, calling us into relationship without the conditional demands of an angry God so many have met through churches.

For Missing Peace to embrace this story and emphasize the counter-cultural without the conditional, we intentionally meet in community space. In our case, a brewery, and invite the whole community. We host it as a potluck and bring in musicians for music and/or Christmas Karaoke and always do our impromptu, messy nativity reenactment.

This is, again, how we attempt radical hospitality. Our version of Christmas Eve is about everyone participating, everyone bringing something, about the miracles in the messes. The perfectly curated performances of Christmas Eve can be beautiful and meaningful, but for some, there is a hunger for something that feels more real, more interactive and authentic. Something that honors a gritty story of a family with no place to go and of meager means. Something that feels more like the life we actually live.

So, we eat together in all the chaos that is for large groups of people with lots of kids. We light candles together and hope for the light in the midst of the darkness as the days of winter begin to lengthen. We do our wild and wooly rendition of the nativity story. We share a few words about what this season means, how we understand it, and we end with vibrant celebrations and merrymaking through song.

Sermon from Christmas Eve at the Brewery

What You Can't Believe About Christmas

https://youtu.be/9LXVqhSdBkM

"Before we join in on the carols and the merrymaking, there's a few things you should know. Prepare yourselves…the story of Christmas as most of us know it, the one our kids just performed, is not likely the reality of the birth of Jesus. I could go into the things lost in translation, but suffice to say, there was likely no stable or inn or innkeeper. There is never a mention of a donkey they rode in on, and the three tellings of this story in scripture conflict about shepherds, wisemen and angels. Sorry to blow this up for you, but what did you expect going to Christmas Eve at a brewery?

But here's the thing. As in all matters of the heart and of the soul, the tangible facts are not the most important part of the story. When you tell the story of your own life, the dates and details won't be what you highlight. It will be about the relationships, the feelings, love and loss, friends and family…at least I hope it will be.

And so it is with this story. This story that invites us into a cultural context that made space for miracles. This story that invites us into the possibility that there not only is a God, but that God loves you and exhibited that by taking the most vulnerable form of a human child. This story that eventually professes a love for this world and its people so great that this innocent child would willingly give his life for it.

Now, I'm okay with it if you struggle with the details...maybe there wasn't a donkey, and likely, it wasn't really a barn, and they might string me up for this one, but I can't even promise Mary was a virgin...but don't let those details stop you from hearing a story of great love, hope, peace and joy. Don't let the things you can't believe stop you from drinking deeply of the promise of a better world and your own role in bringing it about. Don't let cynicism and the fallacy that you can somehow hold on to or control this world by believing the particular brand of truth or reality it is selling inhibit hope and possibility. Because the arch of history may be long, friends, but it bends towards justice. And even if we get large swaths of it wrong, the hope that started with a story of angels and stars and virgin births is right and true and real. Maybe more right and true and real than all the things we can measure and study and prove.

Maybe the things that are most important in this life aren't facts at all, but instead, are the things, the people you love and that love you. And somewhere, deep in the center of who you are, there is a soft hum that resonates with that and knows it as truth. That recognizes the light in me and in you and in the world, that recognizes that arch toward justice, that doesn't ignore the darkness but sees the light more clearly because of it. So this, this time together, this story, these relationships, the good you have the ability to do, all of it...is an invitation to look toward, explore, work with the light of the world, instead of looking at a darkness that is more familiar but holds no promise. I won't say it will be easy, but it will be worth it.

Closing

I cannot tell you how the light comes. What I know is that it is more ancient than imagining. That it travels across an astounding expanse to reach us. That it loves searching out what is hidden, what is lost, what is forgotten or in peril or in pain. That it has a fondness for the body, for finding its way toward flesh, for tracing the edges of form, for shining forth through the eye, the hand, the heart. I cannot tell you how the light comes but that it does. That it will. That it works its way into the deepest dark that enfolds you, though it may seem long ages in coming or arrive in a shape you did not foresee. And so, may we this day turn ourselves toward it. May we lift our faces to let it find us. May we bend our bodies to follow the arc it makes. May we open, and open more and open still to the blessed light that comes"[ix]

By holding loosely some of the beliefs and doctrines around our sacred festivals, we create space. We don't have to let them go, but they can become a conversation instead of a declaration. It is my understanding that our Jewish brothers and sisters tend toward this kind of posture. That scripture is intended to be wrestled with, questioned, even pushed against to grow who we are as a people in light of it because not one of us has all the answers, and even if we did, there'd be no guarantee they'd be the right answers for another.

After the message, we shift right into music and Christmas Karaoke. We lean into the celebrations, joy, family time. A time that jumps right out of the skin of our normal life and brings us acutely into the now together until eyelids become heavy and children become whiney, when we disperse back home for the remainder of each one's personal holiday traditions.

Easter

For Easter, Missing Peace hosts a brunch and egg hunt. Not in addition to worship but as an act of worship. Settling into a meal together, we both acknowledge our needs for nutrition and friendship but also honor and remember the meal Jesus had with his disciples. We often have a champagne toast as part of communion, and joyfully celebrate the resurrection in and with the delight and expectancy the kids experience through their hunt for treats and prizes. Each of these gives us a chance to joyfully experience mystery, hope and new life.

We meet in a historic building that was once a church on the river in Ormond Beach. As people arrive, we set the table for a feast—both the feast of brunch and the holy feast of communion. Everyone joins together to enjoy food around the table, and as folks eat, I share a word about resurrection. The kids will have some kind of craft to keep them occupied while the parents finish eating, and then hide eggs in the park and gardens surrounding our meeting space. And when they are all gleefully hunted and found, we'll close with the voices of the gathered, reflecting on our experience together.

It's an important component of this community's honesty and authenticity to honor what we don't know as well and as frequently as what we do know, and to acknowledge that that grows and changes over time. I love the quote daring us to question our beliefs by asserting "If the you of five years ago doesn't consider the you of today a heretic, you are not growing spiritually."

Sermon from Easter Brunch:

Thank You, Atheists

https://youtu.be/_Ea77OWrZkA

"On this day, we remember the story of a revolutionary who lived 2,000 years ago. He was a man who traveled modern-day Israel, largely on foot, giving people a new narrative. A narrative not ruled by fear, one that is not bound by religious and government regimes of oppression. And the masses thought that sounded pretty good. But as you might imagine, those in power didn't.

So, the powerful plotted and schemed and found a way to be rid of this Jesus. What they didn't realize is that by killing him, they actually made his message all the more real, and further, created an opportunity for him to prove that plots and schemes and oppression do not have the final word. That love and peace and hope Jesus proclaims could defeat even that.

Interestingly, the book of Matthew tells us, when Jesus goes to see his disciples, and I quote, 'When they saw him, they worshipped him, but some doubted.' Some doubted. Even staring Jesus in the face, the story tells us some doubt it. Why record that detail? Why not just tell us that when everyone saw him, they were just overcome with gladness or some Bible-y thing?

But maybe, just maybe, it was to give us hope. Maybe there is some hope wrapped up in our doubt, our fear, our atheism. Here's the thing about atheism, it means questioning. It means we're being honest with our doubt. That we're pushing back against when religion has gone awry and become empirical and oppressive. There is something inside us that says that is not right. And I agree.

Thank you, atheists, for being willing to say that. Thank you for not letting us pretend that everything is OK and ignore that it's not OK. Thank you for telling us not to ignore fraudulent uses of donations and false promises of healing and monsters posing as priests. Thank you, God, for the voices on the outside that are shouting 'we are not living up to Christ.' Thank you. Because sometimes we forget.

Sometimes we get a taste of the power of the divine and we begin to think it's not the divine at all but us. We are powerful. We are in control. And that, my friends, is were evil begins to worm its way in. That's were corruption and hypocrisy and fraud and all the rest get in. And when we start to get our pastors mixed up with God, or pastors begin to get themselves mixed up with God, it sometimes takes someone from the outside calling, 'that's not right!' And they are right; it's not.

Until we are honest, we cannot even begin the conversation. Until we are honest about our failings, until we are honest that we are not God, the church is not God, that God does not live in buildings we build or rituals we create, we don't have a leg to stand on. If you and I are created in the image of God, then so is every atheist, so is every punk kid, so is every evangelist, so is every crook, so is every homeless person, so are we all—believers, doubters and those who are a little of both.

My personal theory is that we are all walking around with a little of both, and it scares the hell out of us. Believers are walking around scared to death that they don't really believe, or that they don't believe all of it, or that they don't believe every day, and that's why some shout their faith so loudly. They are trying to convince themselves as much as you. And on the other side, the atheists are walking around scared to death that they might believe just a little bit. And what if they're wrong? And what if they could be living into something different? What if this whole God thing is real? And it scares the crap out of them. And that's why they shout so loudly that there is no God. They are trying to convince themselves as much as you.

But what if the church were a place where the two, the atheist and the believer, or the atheist and the believer in each of us could be in conversation? What if it were about creating hospitable space to explore what we believe and what we don't believe? To ask hard questions? To wonder together and sometimes wander together? What if that's what church were about? Not convincing either side but looking each other in the face and realizing there's a little of your doubt in my faith and a little of my faith in your doubt. How might we grow? How might we learn if we were willing to face the possibility of the other side?

As the story goes, even those who saw Jesus after the resurrection, like actually saw him, some believed and some doubted. So, why on earth should we think that wouldn't be the same for us 2,000 years later? Or better yet, some mixture of the two. Or even better than that, a living, breathing, growing, changing kind of mixture that continues to question itself and build.

I'm a huge advocate that if you're believing the same thing you believed five years ago, you are trying. You aren't learning. You aren't growing. Come be part of the conversation. Be a witness and let some believe and some doubt. If you notice, Jesus condemns neither. Thank God for that. And let us also not condemn, but instead learn, journey and grow together from the fruitful conversation of the Divine, humanity and the essential ingredient of that relationship. Love. And may we hope. May we hope for the truth in this message that love wins. That the darkness will never extinguish the light. That it will rise again.

There's your takeaway. There is the point of the whole story. Love. And if we're too busy building walls around our belief systems, we cannot love. Spiritual maturity isn't arriving at someplace where you have figured it all out. The maturity comes from being able to sit in the tension of belief and unbelief. Of confidence and doubt. Of divine and human. To sit in that place and grow and learn and explore.

I'm not here to tell you to believe in the Bible. I'm not here to tell you to believe in Christ or God, or any of it. I'm here to be a witness. To create space for conversation. To learn and grow into the reality that each of us holds a divine spark, are created in the Divine image, are children of God. And invite you to hope in a love so great that it comes to earth, conquers death and rises from the dead, because you matter that much. I have no problem believing that you matter that much. Can you believe that you matter that much? Amen."

The hope is to acknowledge our humanity and why that is special. Why we believe each one is special. To highlight the most important pieces of the gospel, the good news. Because, somewhere along the way, the church started making some assumptions about these core truths, that they were understood, and it was time to dive into more doctrinal waters. But who among us doesn't need reminding of our value? That our voice matters and that we are deeply loved?

Messages like these will always be at the core of what it means to be

Missing Peace. We want to teach the things that Jesus taught, live the way Jesus lived, honor the heart of the thing. And we will do this even when it criticizes the institutions and doctrines the church has adopted over the years. Not that we will dismiss or ignore these, we just want space to question them heartily. We want space to think about them in the context of the world we live in now. We want to lower the barriers around them so that we might understand them more fully and access them more completely, regardless of where we stand in our faith, belief or other spiritual journey.

Holy Days Questions:

1. If you imagined the stories of Christmas and Easter in today's context, what would they look like?

2. What are your Christmas and Easter traditions? What in them is sacred and holy?

3. What's at the heart of the thing? What are the most important parts, and are your current traditions and rituals framing that?

4. Why do we need high holy days at all? What do you think is behind the desire for set apart holy time?

CHAPTER 11

A Few Thoughts for Church Leaders

I imagine church folks, like myself, who grew up in church structures, work in church structures, etc. will read this and think, *Well, that's great for Missing Peace, but I could never do that in my church.* Or, if it could be done, may be tempted to merely mimic some of these ideas. And you are welcome to them, but this is not intended to be a magic formula or just a few new ideas. Instead, my hope is that it's about an exploration for you and your people and your context. Where are the places in your community where people are already finding connection and fellowship? Where are people experiencing God, spiritual peace, a sense of awe and wonder? These are your particular clues to what God might be up to in your community. But first, you have to be looking, listening and paying attention to them.

There is a tendency to make assumptions, to think we just know what this group or that wants. Why this group or that doesn't go to church. What would be fun or inviting to folks. You might get lucky and land on something successful and connectional, but the way to be sure of that is to engage the people you hope to reach. Who are these people we want to reach, connect with, invite into deeper relationship with their divine parentage? What is meaningful to them? What do they want for their family, community, world? How do they feel about God, church, faith? What are their stories? And don't guess or assume; ask them!

Once we have the answers to those questions, they are not used to seduce people or to bait folks into coming to something they expressed an interest in. This is not about finding followers or customers but creating relationships and finding ways to journey together. Many of us were raised with a destination-based theology. We behave in this life because of what is promised in the next. It's all about arriving somewhere later. But that's not the Kingdom in, among and with us. The Kingdom Jesus talks about is now.

That means this new way of doing faith isn't about arriving. It's not about getting to membership, baptism or even salvation as defined by church people. Instead, it's about journeying together and genuinely engaging what each—us and other—is learning on their portion of the journey. It's not something we will prepare and curate and deliver. It's an adventure we will take together. A pilgrimage, but through our whole life. We don't get to arrive and then stand at that arrival point yelling to everyone "this way!" We simply all share our stories along the way. And us church folk, part of our story is Jesus and good news and hope and love and however the gospel has changed your life. And if it hasn't, then share that too. Or if you're doubting, or if it's hard, that may be the most relatable part of your story.

Somewhere along the way, we lost touch with part of who Jesus is. The part about standing with the oppressed, the outsider. Seeing value in each one, especially those that society and culture call undesirable and least. And we became more about convincing people they needed church than being the body of Christ at work in the world. Teresa Avila is attributed with saying that Christ has no hands and feet in this world now but ours. But how much do ours look like Jesus'? Are we pushing back against oppressive regimes, speaking truth to power, telling our story and inviting people in? Or have we become oppressive regimes, the power that needs truth spoken to, holding back our story and keeping people out? Perhaps some of both is true. False dichotomies are part of the failure of church, but it's helpful to think about both and find the truth somewhere in it. Pay special attention to where you feel defensive.

It's a clue.

In speaking to churches and mid councils, I've leaned on Luke 10:1-9 to share this call to go and be sent. To lean into the spaces and people of peace and the gifts they bring. To find hope in the midst of the challenge church faces in this age.

Sermon from Black Hawk Presbytery...

There is Hope

https://youtu.be/7C_S1_hEcNA

"In this world, in this day, just what does it look like to take the good news into the

world? It seems like that was pretty clearly defined for a while.

I have these fond memories of growing up in the Presbyterian Church. It has this church smell...it's kinda like old wood and furniture polish and ladies perfume with a bit of must and dust. The preacher wore a robe, always, and as the preacher's kid, I was very familiar with it. I would hide under the back of this robe while he shook hands with all of the congregation...all of the congregation. There was a clear order of worship, a standardized liturgy, organ music, and a precisely timed sermon so we could beat the Baptists to Western Sizzlin'. My hunch is that that sounds familiar to many of you. Yeah, that's what church is. Or perhaps I should say 'was'.

Maybe for some of us, church still looks like those fond memories from a small church in

North Florida. Maybe yours still has those familiar sights smells, and sounds. And maybe, just

maybe, it still has full pews. But increasingly, that's not the case. That church, the one that

generates so much nostalgia for me...one that spawned my call...one that, in my mind, represents "real church" ... one that I love... is dying.

According to Gallup polls, religious "nones" – those who mark none on surveys of religious affiliation, was below 10% in the 80s when my version of "real church" was crystalized. That number now is above 20%. Certainly, the religious landscape of the U.S. is changing. But my hunch is, none of you are sitting there surprised. You've seen it, you've felt it. You remember the days where the potluck was so well attended you hardly took home a scrap of mama's chicken casserole and see the days where you wondered where everyone was as a small group huddled around a table in a largely empty fellowship hall. You remember when the church halls were filled with children's laughter and hoping there might be at least a few for the children's sermon. You've voted on budget cuts with heavy hearts. You've seen churches close and the fights over who's to blame. Perhaps you've succumbed to the hopelessness of it all and wondered if there was anything worth saving...a personal version of Jesus crying out, "O God, O God, why have you forsaken me?"

But it's not all bad news, friends. It may feel like that sometimes, surely it felt like that on the night of Jesus' arrest. Surely the disciples wondered if it was all over when their friend, their teacher, was taken from them, abused and eventually killed. In those final hours, a movement that had reached thousands, that seemed at its peak of hope and healing, dwindled to just a faithful few. But we know something they didn't during those despairing hours. We have the benefit of the rest of the story. A story that tells us the son of God won't stay dead, and neither will his church!

Do not despair, friends, because this is not a story of death but a story of resurrection. And it's already happening. Even in the midst of what seems like the end, we find new beginnings. The 1001 New Worshiping Communities movement of the Presbyterian Church U.S.A. has started 584 faith communities over the last five years. Groups, small and large, are gathering in pubs and beaches and gyms and finding God in unexpected places. They are taking the church outside its walls, and its comfort zone, and finding an abundant harvest. It can feel scary, like being lambs among wolves. We can feel unprepared without our purse or bag or sandals, our usual tools for this kind of journey. But, again and again, we are finding people of peace and sharing our shalom.

Times are changing, there is no doubt about that, but God isn't going anywhere. God is still at work in this world, meeting people where they are and gathering us up. God is still sending laborers into this abundant harvest where Jesus intends to go. And the incarnational work, the hands-on, head-in, heart-filled work of the gospel carries on, building the Kingdom and announcing each one's identity as a beloved child of God created in God's image. And that, my friends, is good news.

I hope that that message lightens your heart a bit. But I also hope that it calls you to action. God bless Blackhawk Presbytery and your theme of God's mission has a church because it does, and it's true, and it's me and it's you that are part of how that all plays out. We each have gifts and a role in what the resurrected church looks like. Not any one person, but all of us together. We've long said the church is the body of Christ, we've long said we are the church. It's time to move our body, friends! It's time to use our abundant gifts for God's purpose. Even if it looks different than we expected. Even if it's in unusual places and with unusual people; perhaps, especially if it is. That's the way Jesus did it.

Teresa Avila, a 16th century monastic said, "Christ has no body now but yours. No hands, no feet on earth but yours. Yours are the eyes through which he looks compassion on this world. Yours are the feet with which he walks to do good. Yours are the hands through which he blesses all the world. Yours are the hands, yours are the feet, yours are the eyes, you are his body. Christ has no body now on earth but yours." And it's as true now as it was then...maybe even more so.

So, what will we do? How do we go forward? You are fortunate to be part of a Presbytery exploring those questions and part of a denomination investing in and creating tools to help us discover it. But beware of simple answers, friends. Just as the kingdom of God is deep and wide and diverse, just as God reveals Godself in so many different ways, so may the future of church look and feel and be.

But you are the believers. You are the church. You already know where God is. You already have experienced the grace of the gospel and the deep and wide love of God. Where? How? What's it like?

And what would it be like to share that?

Feel like lambs among wolves a bit? But if we don't trust this message and the God it comes from, then who will? So, we have to share it. We have to partner with our divine parent and in this work. Because we are the body. We are the hands and feet. We are the eyes and ears and mouth. And not one of us is alone. The harvest is plentiful. There is much to do, friends. But because of who we are and who's we are, we are up to the task. Rise up, Blackhawk Presbytery! It may feel like Friday, but we already know Sunday is coming! Take what time you need in the tomb, but don't stay there. Our story doesn't end there. Pray for more laborers for the harvest, and be those laborers too, and fear not, because this place…this place that can seem like it's all too much and the harvest is too great, this is the place where Christ intends to go.

Amen."

Our story, the one that draws us into relationship with God through Christ, the one that brings hope and life, the one that draws us into the next place God is sending us, is not one of death but of resurrection. But we don't get to skip over the death part. And that doesn't mean we can't begin to listen to the call to resurrection at the same time.

After this sermon, I asked the participants of Black Hawk Presbytery to answer some questions. I asked them, "Where do people gather in your community?" And then asked, "What would it look like to bring church to that space?" They had lovely ideas and answers. Things they knew in their heart, things they were dreaming in their spirit, maybe even called to, but didn't know they could do or felt they needed permission.

If this work is anything, let it be a permission slip to follow where God is calling. To try things. To fail along the way…or what may feel like failure…but we see what God does with things that feel like failure, that feel like death. God resurrects them! God is about life where we see no life at all. God is about hope where all seems hopeless. God is about light in the darkness. And we, the followers of this God, have to be the ones to see it…to see the life, the hope, the light. If not us, who? If not now, when?

If you're feeling a little lost or overwhelmed, good. That's part of our story too. May it not be 40 years lost and wandering, but in our lostness is often where we are formed (or re-formed?), are found.

A Sermon on lostness

Lost and Found

https://youtu.be/XKumveiWJBM

"Do you ever feel lost? Unsure of what step to take next. Unsure whether to stay or go. Wondering if it's time for a major change or stay the course. And how do you know? And who has time to even think about that? And have I done any of the steps right so far? And how can I be sure?

I'm serious. Have you ever felt this way? I'll wait…

Thanks for letting me know it's not just me. And now I hope you know it's not just you.

For me, this plays out like moments of peace and confidence and energy, and I plow ahead at full speed. Full of an idea and hope and dreams, and the pedal goes to the metal for as long as I can. But at some point, it's time to refuel. And you can ask Jeff, I always wait 'til the last drop. And then I wonder why I'm so empty and tired and start wondering if everything I've done was wrong and my confidence and peace was all a façade, and all that energy was for not. Then, usually, I get a little rest, a little prayer, a little hope and start again…often following the same pattern.

I've just recently become aware of this pattern...maybe just as recently as writing it down...but I've realized it's not just my pattern. That some version of it is present in the ancient stories of scripture, and in the people around me, and even in nature.

There's this cool, old professor from Columbia Seminary, where I attended for a short time, who is bold and cusses and is a bit curmudgeon-y but says these amazing things about the old testament. He brings it to life in really incredible ways, and if you are curious about that, look up Walter Bruggemann. Anyway, he categorizes the psalms in these categories of orientation, disorientation and reorientation. Just like my pattern, these ancient poems are snapshots of people's experience of a sort of normalcy, a lostness, and then a new normal. Hopefully, a better normal with more experience and knowledge behind it (God, let that be so).

It's got me thinking that if we can start to recognize our patterns, we can learn all the more from them. Learn ways of finding peace in our lostness instead of panic. Resting assured that something follows the lostness. Maybe that will give us a bit more compassion for ourselves, and Brené Brown—an expert on empathy and compassion—says that's the first step into having real empathy for others.

To be clear, she draws a stark line between sympathy and empathy. We aren't talking about the "I feel so bad for you" kind of motivation. That's not connecting. That's holding at arm's length and even kind of looking down on this pitiful thing in this pitiful situation. We do this to our own pain even...hold it at arm's length, look down on it like some sad, sappy thing that's not really part of us, or just needs to be powered through, or maybe even superficially soothed or numbed.

But the tendency then is to do that to others, look down at those pitiful people in their pitiful situation, some sad, sappy thing. They just need to power through. Or let's do some surface-level soothing and then tell ourselves we did our part. So, how is that not what we're doing?

Can we let it really penetrate us? Reach into our hearts and begin a little empathy for our patterns, for our lostness, for our disorientation. If we can, then it becomes about authentic change, at a minimum for you yourself and me myself. It's not about never feeling lost or overwhelmed—that's a part of the journey and has been for thousands of years if we look at these ancient stories and poems, but can we...can we be gentle in it? Can we love ourselves and others even in the midst of it all?

A friend recently invited me when I feel sad to imagine my sadness as a person, someone I could sit next to, just be with, talk to. And at first, it was hard...really scary. I didn't want to see myself that way. Depressed, depleted, sad. No one wants to be around this gloomy version of hopelessness. Until that point, I hadn't really realized the intense sadness I was capable of. And I didn't want to know. It felt like a dark hole I could fall into and never come out of. But I tried again. I imagined myself hugging sad-me. I told her it was okay to be sad, and I'd just sit with her if she wanted. I told her I was sorry I ignored her and saw her sadness as weakness. Her pain as unimportant and insignificant. The ways I tried to convince her to just suck it up and keep going. I told her she could just be sad, and I wouldn't abandon her.

This is not a conversation I can have just once. It's going to take more than that. But something did release a bit. Something lifted. And I feel a new compassion for myself and other people experiencing depression...something, if I'm honest, I'd been dismissive of and mad at.

It's hard to grow, friends. It's hard to feel. It's incredibly hard to feel lost. It feels dangerous. But you know that, cause you've done it. And you survived. You traveled from your oriented through your disoriented and came out reoriented a new way. And you'll do it again. You're doing it now. This is the way we will grow and transform. No magic pill, no magic religion, no magic relationship. Just normal, lost, new normal. Just caterpillar, cocoon, butterfly. Just sure, unsure, sure again. But here's what you need to know: you can do this. Many have before, and many more will. You have.

And what if everyone we pitied or shamed or looked down on—the other in an issue, the other political party, someone we've labeled foolish, someone we've labeled weak, someone we've labeled hurtful—what if we could see them with an empathy that we extend to ourselves and to others? To that foolish or weak or hurtful person inside us, and the one we see out there. Because when we want to punish ourselves, we want to punish others too.

So, that's how what we're doing isn't just pity and sympathy. Because we are walking together through whatever version of disorientation we are in, and in doing so, becoming along the way. And when we change ourselves, not one thing we interact with can stay the same. The formula changes. So, can you be compassionate to yourself in your lostness? Because that's how you'll have genuine compassion for anyone else. Can you look at that sad, hurting or angry person in yourself and give them a hug? Tell them it will be okay, not as a platitude, but because you know; you've done it before and you have this book of thousands of confessions of others who have, and you have this community that is each one and together doing it too. God, let it be so. Amen."

Fear not, friends. It's beckoned to us in 365 places in scripture, old and new testaments, from thousands and thousands of years and millions and millions of people…fear not. Listen well, follow your calling, fail and get lost, and then found again.

Ultimately my "how-to" is about listening and then trying things. Listen first to the voices of the people you want to reach. Listen to what they think about God. What they long for. Where they are experiencing a sense of spiritual peace, awe, wonder, hope. And meet them in those spaces. It isn't hard to find God and the gospel in the midst of awe, wonder and hope.

Then try things based on what you've learned, and share what you believe, what you've found in scripture. Why your faith is important to you. But not as if your way is the only way. If we share what we know to be true in a fashion that requires all other ideas to be wrong, we will surely fail. How do we meet people where they are, on the fertile ground of where folks are already experiencing goodness, God-ness, and really journey together, honoring each other and where we are/what we've learned on our journey?

Missionaries, dating back to Paul, have always had to learn the language of the people they hope to reach. The same is true for us now. What language can you use to describe your faith and belief that's understandable to the outsider? Can you answer *why* or *what does that mean* multiple times around a statement of what you believe to be true? This will help distill it into something easily understood by the masses.

Perhaps, an example, if you say, "I believe in Jesus because he is our salvation," (a classic Christian belief statement) then answer, *what does that mean?* You might say, "It means our salvation is in servant leadership, in the first being the last and last being first. In shedding the cultural norms of consumerism and productivity for ones that serve and love and care for self and others. And this is what Jesus taught us and showed us through his life, right up to the sacrifice of it." Or however you would answer that, but authentically and clearly and in language that can be understood. You may have to answer *what does that mean* or *why* multiple times to get to your distilled version, but you'll get to it.

Sometimes, I think the church hides behind theological and doctrinal language. Then we never have to dig deep and explain what we think, feel and believe, or we are afraid to be wrong. But this is also where grace and humility come in. And that is a super helpful place to start a deep conversation about the Divine, the self and what they have to do with each other.

I believe the mistakes we make, the messiness of this life, is often where God shows up most powerfully. The unexpected places, the things out of our control, the unusual are where we can find grace. So, when a pink-haired mermaid shows up, you can swaddle her and put her in the starring role, and the nativity still happens. God shows up. People are engaged, and dare I say, transformed. Because of, in spite of, or just alongside a pink-haired mermaid baby Jesus. Amen.

Discussion Questions for Church Leaders:

1. Where do people gather in your community? Why?

2. What is good news in those places?

3. Where is the need in your community?

4. Who can you talk to outside the church about what they believe?

5. Make a statement about what you believe. Is it understandable? Can you "why" it down to something that is?

EPILOGUE

How Does It feel to Do This?

There is something undeniable, unavoidable and holy happening in this world all the time. If we will only take the time to stop and listen, to pay attention deeply—both to our personal experience of it, the stories of others' experience of it and the experience we share in community. When we do this Missing Peace thing, it's not about the next hip version of church. It's not about convincing each other or religious institution or our community. Instead, it's about deep, moving, transformational experience of the Divine, so palpable and meaningful that to not share it is to burst trying to contain it. If church were that, who could reject it?

In my imagination, you dear reader, are inspired. You have ideas and steps forming for how you might engage the divine in community. And ideas are lovely, and perfect, and beautiful, but the moment they become reality…the moment they take on flesh…they become something else. In a conversation I had with Rob Bell, he called this kenotic involution—a willing emptying of self and abandoning the perfect, awesome, borderless-ness in order for there to actually be a thing instead of just an idea. In order for there to be an actual gathering, book, class, experience—whatever happens, there must be the actual doing. It can never be all that it was in the idea, but it can be real and lived.

In that same conversation, Rob Bell talked about a friend of his who would have a funeral for each of his ideas before he experienced the first cut of it. He had to let the idea die so that the reality could happen. He had to release all the perfection, all the expectation and let it be what it was going to be instead of just remaining his idea of what it would be.

Before starting Missing Peace, I told my husband, "I feel like I'm running toward a cliff and God is saying, 'Jump!' and I'm saying, 'Jump? I can't jump! It's a freaking cliff!'" And Jeff looks at me and says, "Katy, you've already jumped."

It will feel a bit like jumping. It will feel a bit like a funeral. To live into these callings and ideas is both to die and to really, truly live. Not unlike the radical story of a subversive, revolutionary Rabbi who lived a couple thousand years ago. We church folk are often implored to "be like Jesus." Here's the invitation. May we be radical, incarnational, subversive revolutionaries.

Make the thing you feel called to make—and not for someone else; for you—because your life would be less than lived if you didn't. And if it happens to be meaningful for someone else, "Grace upon grace"(Ephesians 3:18-19).

If you do actually decide to make the thing, to let the word take on flesh, it may feel like a great, big emptying of self. It did for me. And it took me a while to figure out that the answer to that empty feeling was not to just work harder and do more and try to get results, but instead to do the things that make more Katy. This is how I'll be enough, not by what I produce or how people respond to it, or strategic plans or any of that.

In that same conversation with Rob Bell, he invited us to actually live the experience we curate. "Be willing to be surprised in public." Actually live the experience out, and let it be what it is. Release it from your expectations and metrics that can rob it of the life. Let it live and witness and enjoy what comes from it.

This idea makes me think of creation. God let the word take on flesh, breathed into humanity, and then let us be free to see what would become of God's best ideas. What if we could do the same? Maybe this is what it means to be made in the Divine image. That we, too, can breathe life into ideas; that we, too, can bring Spirit into form.

May it be so.

Sources

---

i https://www.kyudo.com/kyudo-k.html
ii https://www.bible.com/bible/111/HEB.10.24-25.NIV
iii Influenced by Rob Bell's Everything is Spiritual: https://youtu.be/i2rklwkm_dQ
iv https://onbeing.org/civil-conversations-project/
v https://arcvolusia.org/
vi Poem by Theresa Avila:
https://www.journeywithjesus.net/PoemsAndPrayers/Teresa_Of_Avila_Christ_Has_No_Body.shtml
vii Genesis 23:4, Deuteronomy 10:19, Leviticus 19:34, Leviticus 27:19, 1 Chronicles 16:19-22, Job 29:15-17, Psalm146:9, Jeremiah 7:5-7, Ezekiel 47:22, Zechariah 7:9-10, Matthew 5:43-44, Matthew 25:35, etc
viii https://www.heschel.org/academics/lower-school/lower-school-updates/lower-school-news/~board/ls-updates/post/early-childhood-and-lower-school-children-come-together-for-a-martin-luther-king-jr-assembly
ix https://emilierichards.com/2019/01/06/sunday-inspiration-how-the-light-comes/

Made in the USA
Monee, IL
20 November 2020